DATE			

TELFORD'S BRITAIN

TELFORD'S
BRITAIN
Derrick Beckett

DAVID & CHARLES
Newton Abbot   London   North Pomfret (Vt)

FOR SALLY

Line illustrations by Malcolm Kaye

British Library Cataloguing in Publication Data
Beckett, Derrick
 Telford's Britain.
 1. Telford, Thomas 2. Civil engineering
 ——Great Britain——History
 I. Title
 624   TA140.T3

 ISBN 0–7153–8588–7

Typeset by ABM Typographics Limited, Hull
and printed in Great Britain
by Butler & Tanner Limited, Frome and London
for David & Charles Publishers plc
Brunel House Newton Abbot Devon

Published in the United States of America
by David & Charles Inc
North Pomfret Vermont 05053 USA

PREFACE

In many different fields of activity, a relatively small number of individuals living within the span of the past two centuries exerted a massive influence which has continued to this day. This is certainly the case with regard to the development of transportation systems, and the contribution of Thomas Telford (1757–1834) is arguably at least the equal of that of the Stephensons and the Brunels. The careers of Robert Stephenson (1803–59) and Isambard Kingdom Brunel (1806–59) ran in parallel and their primary contribution to transportation was associated with the railway era between 1830 and 1859. Brunel, of course, made an immense contribution to the development of ship construction in addition to his work on railways.

Telford was over seventy when George and Robert Stephenson had established the viability of the steam locomotive and track as a reliable means of transportation, with the opening of the Liverpool and Manchester Railway in 1830. By the time of Telford's death in 1834, Robert Stephenson was grappling with the construction of the embankments, cuttings, tunnels and bridges on the 112 mile (180km) London and Birmingham Railway and Isambard Kingdom Brunel had been appointed engineer to the proposed 118 mile (190km) Great Western Railway between London and Bristol. Telford's involvement with railways was limited but significant and his primary contribution to transportation was in the construction of roads and canals. The impact of railways on roads and canals was immediate and severe: within two and a half years of the opening of the Liverpool and Manchester Railway, the number of coaches plying between the two cities was reduced from twenty-nine to one. Soon after, steam locomotives were able to haul loads several times heavier than by a horse-drawn canal barge. Thus Telford's contribution to transportation has tended to be overshadowed by the subsequent works of the Victorian railway engineers; in particular Brunel's charisma, productivity, flair and attention to architectural detail have attracted immense interest, culminating in the 150th anniversary celebrations of commencement of work on the Great Western Railway. This needs to be put in context: at the time of Brunel's birth, Telford was working on civil engineering projects which, in relative terms, were of equal magnitude to current proposals for a Channel crossing. Shortly after Brunel had completed his formal education, Telford had built the world's largest span bridge, the Menai Suspension Bridge, which was opened in 1826. Telford's works — docks, canals, roads — extend from London to the north of Scotland, and the primary aim of this book (as with *Brunel's Britain* and *Stephensons' Britain*) is to chronicle Telford's engineering works as they exist today and to examine their technical and architectural merit. A comprehensive gazetteer is included in the hope of encouraging the reader to visit Telford's works in England, Wales and Scotland.

DERRICK BECKETT, London

CONTENTS

Youths of respectability and competent education who contemplate Civil Engineering as a profession are seldom aware how far they ought to descend in order to found the basis of future elevation. Not only are the natural senses of seeing and feeling requisite in the examination of materials, but also the practised eye and the hand which has experience of the kind and qualities of stone, of lime, of iron, of timber and even of earth and of the effects of human ingenuity in applying and combining all these substances is necessary for arriving at mastery in the profession: for how can a man give judicious directions unless he possesses personal knowledge of the details requisite to effect his ultimate purpose in the best and cheapest manner? It has happened to me more than once, when taking opportunities of being useful to a young man of merit, that I have experienced opposition in taking him from his books and drawings and placing a mallet, chisel or trowel in his hand, till rendered confident by the solid knowledge which experience can only bestow, he was qualified to insist on the due performance of workmanship, and to judge of merit in the lower as well as the higher departments of a profession in which no kind of degree of practical knowledge is superfluous. For this reason, I ever congratulate myself upon the circumstances which impelled me to begin by working with my own hands, and thus to acquire early experience of the habits and feelings of workmen; it being equally important to the Civil Engineer, as to Naval or Military Commanders to have passed through all the grades of their profession.

The Life of Thomas Telford by T. Telford 1838, ed. John Rickman

INTRODUCTION
ROADS, CANALS AND BRIDGES

Roads

Shortly before Thomas Telford was born, a cartoon of the period depicted a sailor with a wooden leg beside a stage coach. Asked whether he wants a lift, he replies: 'No, I am in a hurry.' This was indicative of the appalling state of the roads in Britain about the middle of the eighteenth century. In fact, fourteen to eighteen hundred years previously, Britain possessed a far superior road network due to the enterprise of the Romans. Prior to the expeditions of Julius Caesar in 55–54 BC, Britain possessed a meandering system of narrow roads and trackways and there was extensive use of broad-wheeled waggons for the transport of goods. For the rapid communications necessary for military purposes, the Romans planned and built a comprehensive network of roads and their extent can be fully appreciated by reference to the Ordnance Survey Map of Roman Britain. Amongst the more significant roads were Ermine Street from London via Lincoln and York to the River Tay in Scotland, Fosse Way from Exeter to Bath, Cirencester, Leicester and Lincoln, and Watling Street from Dover to London, St Albans and Chester. Telford's improvements to the London and Holyhead road (A5(T)) follow in part the route of Watling Street. The Romans made little impact on Scotland and it was left to General George Wade and subsequently Telford to build a comprehensive network of roads north of Hadrian's Wall. As with their bridge building, the Romans adopted a professional approach to road construction. The line of the road was set out by means of posts and pegs and for the more important routes two parallel trenches were excavated along the edges of the formation and the top soil and loose material removed, down to firm strata. A layer of fine, well-compacted soil (pavinmentum) was placed on the firm strata. Above this was placed a layer of fitted flat stones (statumen) followed by the rudus, a crude form of concrete consisting of broken stones and lime. The top two layers were the nucleus, consisting of small broken stones or tiles or gravel, and the dorsum, which consisted of fitted stones of rectangular or polygonal form. The top surface was cambered and raised well above the surrounding ground level, to ensure that water ran off the dorsum into the adjacent ditches. Thus it can be seen that these roads were properly engineered, and many have lasted two thousand years. These roads were built up to 15ft (4.6m) wide, allowing two waggons or chariots to pass one another. The legions marched six abreast and two were able to pass one another without breaking step.

The Romans left Britain about AD 407 and subsequently road building fell into a rapid decline. In the medieval period some road and bridge building was undertaken by the monasteries, and the principal means of transporting goods was by way of the pack-horse and small carts. As trade within England and with the Continent developed, the need for improved roads and vehicles increased. The first coaches were in use by 1555 and about the same time passenger waggons travelling at about 2mph plied between London and a few towns in south-east England. An Act of Parliament was passed in 1555, dealing with the upkeep of roads. Parishes were made responsible for the maintenance of their own roads and every villager was required to do six days' unpaid work on the roads each year (R. Syme). The Act proved to be unworkable and in an attempt to reduce further deterioration of the roads, an Act of 1621 forbade the use of carrying a load of more than 1 ton (20kN). Coach services were introduced in the 1630s.

The first of a number of Turnpike Acts was passed in 1663 with the purpose of making travellers pay a toll for use of the roads. Toll-houses were set up at intervals along the roads, together with wooden barriers with iron spikes, referred to as pikes (the origin of the expression 'turnpike'). By the early eighteenth century, there were several thousand turnpikes in England but there was no significant improvement in the roads, and an expression of public feeling at the time was '. . . From Grimsthorpe to Colsterworth are 8 miles, called by courtesy of the neighbourhood a Turnpike, but in which we were every moment either buried in quagmires of mud or racked to dislocation by pieces of rock which they term mending . . .' (R. Syme).

As the population of towns increased, there was an ever-growing need for reliable coach services, but the proprietors were severely hampered by the state of the roads and journey times were often prefixed by 'if God permits' — the coach journey from London to Edinburgh could take fourteen days.

It will be recalled that the Romans were unable to develop a comprehensive network of roads in Scotland as they did in England, but it was in Scotland that the first engineered roads were built since the Roman era, again largely for military purposes. Following the Jacobite risings, General George Wade (1673–1748) was appointed commander of forces in northern Britain and over a period of eleven years built 250 miles of roads in Scotland and numerous bridges (see also Chapter 8). An old epigram (S. Smiles) ran: 'Had you seen these roads before they were made, You'd lift up your hands and bless General Wade'. The form of construction was similar to that used by the Romans. The principal routes were: along the line of the Great Glen of Scotland close to the line of the Caledonian Canal (see Chapter 7); a second connected Fort Augustus with Dunkeld via Blair Atholl; and a third connected Fort George with Coupar Angus via Badenoch and Braemar.

In England, John Metcalf (1717–1810), a remarkable personality, made a significant contribution to the improvement of communications by road in Lancashire and Yorkshire. Metcalf was born at Knaresborough and at the age of six contracted smallpox and was blinded for life. He worked as a musician, a soldier in General Wade's army, chapman, fish dealer, horse dealer and waggoner. About 1765, 'Blind Jack' turned to road building and over a period of 30 years he was responsible for the construction of about 180 miles of turnpike roads, which involved the construction of numerous bridges, retaining walls and culverts. He developed a technique of constructing roads over boggy ground by providing a formation of bundles of heather placed in rows in alternate directions, above which was placed a layer of stone and gravel. George Stephenson used a similar technique when constructing the Liverpool and Manchester Railway over Chat Moss.

Between 1775 and 1830 there was considerable improvement in the technique of road construction with important contributions from a French engineer, Pierre Tresaquet (1716–94), John Loudon McAdam (1756–1836) and Thomas Telford (1757–1834). Fig 1 shows the construction details of various road designs; Tresaquet's system was generally adopted in France and other parts of Europe and influenced the work of Telford and McAdam.

McAdam claimed to be a road repairer rather than road builder and was more interested in the road surface than the route it followed. It can be seen (Fig 1) that in contrast to Telford he did not use large stones, and the soil was excavated to convex form to ensure that water flowed off the finished surface. He stressed the importance of keeping the soil under the construction dry:

That it is the native soil which really supports the weight of traffic; that while it is preserved in a dry state, it will carry any weight without sinking and that it does in fact carry the road and carriages also; that this native soil must be previously made quite dry and a covering impenetrable to rain must then be placed over it in that dry state; that the thickness of the road should only be regulated by the quantity of material necessary to form such impervious covering and never by any reference to its own power of carrying weight.

Fig 1 Construction details of various road designs

Section of typical Roman road, showing footing of compacted earth, waterproof layer of small stones, base course of Roman concrete, cambered middle course of local hard filling, and wearing course of local materials. Note retaining stones A and draining ditch B

Tresaquet's pavement design, the precursor of the modern road. Heavy stones laid on a cambered footing with similar layer of large stones, topped with a wearing surface of small stones.

Telford's design for road pavements. Foundation of heavy flat stones, laid direct on levelled topsoil, a two-layer cambered base of small stones, deeper in the centre, and a wearing surface of clean gravel

McAdam's simple but effective road pavement, a wearing surface and base course comprising three layers of small stones laid on a compacted cambered footing

Although modern road engineers would agree with McAdam's views on making the road impervious, the construction thickness would be related to the intensity of loading and the nature of the ground on which the road is built. McAdam's system was cheaper than Telford's and of particular use for the repair and construction of older roads. He was appointed surveyor general of roads in 1827 and the macadam road system became widely used in Europe and America. In relation to road construction, McAdam's name is far better known than Telford's, but the London and Holyhead road, constructed between 1815 and 1830, remains largely as built by Telford, and this includes a number of major bridges. The London and Holyhead road is described in Chapter 4.

Canals

The inadequacy of Britain's road system in the sixteenth to eighteenth centuries hindered, as we have seen, the efficient operation of coach services and the movement of goods. As an alternative to the hazardous nature of transport of goods by road, pack-horses were taken down to the nearest navigable river and loaded on to barges. The River Severn, for example, generated extensive traffic, and towns such as Worcester, Bewdley and Bridgnorth became thriving ports for the transport of goods to and from the Midlands. The River Severn, as we shall see, has close associations with the life of Thomas Telford, and between 1790 and 1830 he constructed six bridges over the river, including those at Worcester and Bewdley (see Chapter 2).

Although rivers attracted population growth in their immediate vicinity, their meandering routes involved long and hazardous journeys between towns and villages and further, their slope, rapid variations in water depth and flow and obstructions made navigation over long stretches impossible. There was an obvious need for controlling the flow of water in rivers and to use water power to drive water-wheels for corn mills. In the Domesday Book of the eleventh century, over 5,000 water-mills were recorded. Mills were built on river banks and weirs (river dams) were constructed to raise the upper level of the stream. This provided sufficient pressure to power the water-wheels and increased the depth of navigation. However, the weir formed a barrier to navigation and this was overcome by providing a means of opening part of the weir, achieved by the use of 'flash' locks. A flash lock was a gateway in a weir consisting of a series of planks that slotted into position on top of each other. To let a boat pass through the weir, the timber planks were removed and a boat travelling downstream could 'flash' through. It was a different matter for boats plying upstream against the flow and they were hauled through the gap by ropes from the river bank. As the majority of weirs were constructed for the convenience of the mill owners, the operation of the water-wheels took precedence over navigation. Opening of the flash lock meant losing the head of water to power the mill, and thus there was conflict between the millers and the boat owners. This often resulted in considerable delays, making inland water transport slow and tedious. It is recorded that flash locks existed on the River Thames from about 1200. From a navigational point of view, a more satisfactory means of converting a river from a slope to, in effect, a series of horizontal levels with connecting vertical steps, was achieved with the introduction of 'pound' locks, the lock-free section of water between two locks being known as the pound. These were built near weirs and consisted of a chamber with gates at each end, the features of which are shown in Fig 2. Early pound locks were fitted with gates which lifted vertically (guillotine gates) and were used on the Grand Canal in China, c800. The water in the lock could be raised or lowered by means of sluices to the level at which the boat was floating. The gate at the boat end was then opened and the boat moved into the chamber. The gate was closed and the water within the chamber was raised or lowered until it reached the level at which the boat was able to continue its journey up or down the river. Fig 2 shows progress downstream. It should be noted that the gate at the downstream end of a lock has to retain a greater height of water and thus pressure. The unit weight of water is about 62lb per cubic foot ($10kN/m^3$) and the pressure increases in a linear manner with height. Thus if the height of the gate is, say, 20ft (6.1m), the pressure at the bottom will be $62 \times 20 = 1,240lb/ft^2$ ($61kN/m^2$). This results in a total force of 12,400lb/ft width of the gate

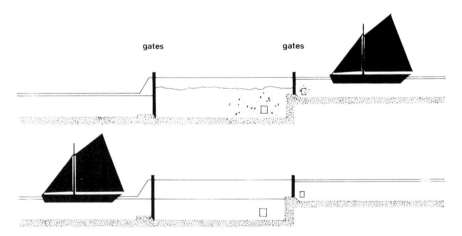

Fig 2 Details of a pound lock

186kN/m). Thus the gates and the walls of the lock chamber have to resist substantial forces. The design of the first lock with mitred swinging gates which, when closed, formed a 'V' against the pressure of the water, is attributed to Leonardo da Vinci. He designed a lock of this type at San Marco, Italy, circa 1500.

In parallel with the improvement of river navigation, artificial waterways (canals) were constructed where there were no rivers suitable for boats, or sections of rivers were connected with canals by forming lateral cuts where navigation was not possible.

Following the construction of the Grand Canal in China, there were significant developments in hydraulic engineering in Italy. As with the construction of roads and bridges referred to elsewhere, the military influence was strong. The reconstruction of Milan's defences in the twelfth century included new city walls and a large moat (W. B. Parsons). To supply water to the moat, the Naviglio Grande was constructed to supply water from the River Ticino, some 16 miles (26km) away. In the next two centuries, further canals were built in the vicinity of Milan and short canals connected to the moat were run into the city.

The Romans constructed the first artificial navigations in Britain, such as the Foss Dyke between the Trent and Witham at Lincoln. As with roads, there was little further development following the departure of the Romans for several hundred years. The first pound locks in England were constructed on a lateral cut running alongside the River Exe, known as the Exeter Canal, which was built between 1564 and 1567.

The most notable canal construction in the seventeenth century can be attributed to Sir Richard Western (1591–1652). He engineered the Wey Navigation from the Thames at Weybridge to Guildford. It fell 86ft (26.3m) between Guildford and the Thames and in a distance of 15 miles (24km) there were 7 miles (11km) of artificial cuts. Construction of the navigation, which was completed in 1653, required 10 pound locks, 12 bridges and 4 weirs. It retains a number of original features including a partly turf-sided pound lock at New Haw. At Byfleet there is an interesting juxtaposition of transportation systems: the junction with the Basingstoke Canal (1794), the London and Southampton Railway (1840) and the M25 motorway (1984). The M25 straddles the Wey Navigation and the railway.

The first modern canals in England were built in the second half of the eighteenth century. In 1753, Henry Berry (1720–1812) surveyed Sankey Brook with the intention of making it navigable between the Mersey and St Helens. An Act for the work was passed in 1755 and Berry proposed that it would be preferable to construct a canal with water supply from the brook. The canal, 10 miles (16km) in length, with nine locks providing a fall of 78ft (24m), was completed in 1757. It was essentially a lateral cut, running parallel to the line of the brook and could be considered as the transition between a navigable river and a canal which was independent of any river. The Duke of Bridgewater (1736–1803) is generally given the credit for the first modern English canal. The duke employed pack-horses, at considerable expense, to transport coal from his Worsley pits. Thus commercial reasons resulted in an Act to construct a 34 mile (54km) long canal which provided a more economic means of transporting coal from the duke's estate. The Bridgewater Canal between Worsley and Runcorn was opened in 1772 and was engineered by James Brindley (1716–72). Brindley was also engineer for the Trent and Mersey Canal, which was completed five years after his death (see Chapter 1).

The water supply for the Bridgewater Canal was obtained in part from the drainage of colliery workings. The canal was lock-free but there were formidable engineering problems, including an aqueduct over the River Irwell at Barton, which was preceded by a 2,700ft (825m) embankment. Construction was carried out by hand with primitive tools, and the workers were called 'navigators', the derivation of the term 'navvy'. For making the canal bed watertight, Brindley used the puddle clay technique. The excavation was lined with puddle: a suitable mix of clay and water which was trampled by foot to achieve the correct consistency. Despite the Duke of Bridgewater's massive investment in the project, it was a notable financial success, the cost of transporting coal being a fraction of that by pack-horse.

Table 1

	Tons	kN
Pack-horse	0.125	1.25
Stage waggon, soft road	0.625	6.25
Stage waggon, macadam road	2.0	20.0
Waggon on rails	8.0	80.0
Barge on river	30.0	300.0
Barge on canal	50.0	500.0

In a similar manner to the impact of the completion of Iron Bridge on the subsequent use of cast iron as a construction material for bridges, the Bridgewater Canal intensified interest in the potential of canals as an alternative to transporting goods by road. Table 1 (A. W. Skempton), which gives average figures derived from a number of authorities, including Telford and Smeaton, gives typical loads carried or drawn by a single horse. The advantage of the horse-drawn canal barge is immediately apparent, but unfortunately the majority of English canals proved too small, compared with canals built in Europe, to carry large loads economically. With the development of the railways from 1830 onwards, the British Canal system fell into rapid decline and is now used primarily and successfully for leisure purposes.

Important canals with which Telford was associated, in particular the Ellesmere Canal (Chapter 3) and the Birmingham and Liverpool Junction Canal (Chapter 1) are 'narrow canals' and the size of boats is limited to about 70ft (21m) by 7ft (2.1m), governed by the lock size.

In contrast to the Bridgewater Canal, these canals required the construction of numerous locks and a major consideration was the supply of water. Typical features of canals are shown in Fig 3. The locks act as steps between a series of levels and occasionally several locks were built close together and are known as staircase locks. A notable example is the flight of eight locks on Telford's Caledonian Canal (not a narrow canal; see Chapter 7), referred to as 'Neptune's Staircase'. Every time a lock is used, water is taken from the pound above, and the larger the lock the greater the volume of water used — thus the preference for narrow locks on early canals. Reservoirs (Fig 3), were the most common source of water supply and water was also pumped in from local rivers. Designs

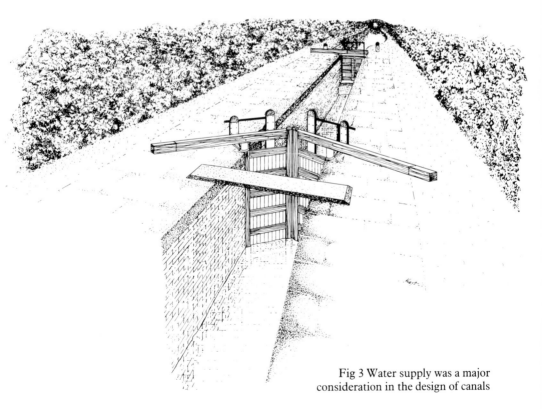

Fig 3 Water supply was a major consideration in the design of canals

by Telford (*Telford's Atlas*) for narrow lock gates are shown in Plate 1. In the upper diagram, the top timber gate is single and extends to the full width of the lock chamber (the head of water to be resisted at the top end is lower than at the bottom end). The bottom end resists a greater head of water and twin mitred gates are used. The cast-iron gates in the lower diagram are mitred at the top and bottom of the chamber for ease of fabrication and lifting. The more spectacular aspects of Telford's canals are described in Chapters 1, 3 and 7.

Bridges

Bridges form an essential part of transportation systems — roads, canals and railways — and their function is to provide a passageway for people, vehicles or materials, both solid and liquid, where normal surface construction is not practical. It is this singleness of purpose that distinguishes a bridge from other forms of structure. The design of building structures, for example, involves several variables — spatial requirements, heating, ventilation, lighting and so on — and in many instances structure will not be the dominant factor. In a bridge, structure dominates and its form should reflect this. The essence of an elegant bridge is simplicity of line, in which the structural form is expressed to the full. The addition of superfluous features will in general detract from the beauty of a bridge rather than enhance it. This simplicity of line is as necessary in the design of a simple footbridge over a stream as in the structure of a bridge for a major river crossing.

A bridge should be designed to blend with the landscape rather than compete with it. It has been said that it is difficult to make a bridge look ugly, but this has frequently been achieved by the incorporation of heavy parapets and unnecessary ornamentation. It could be argued that Telford did not construct an ugly bridge, and throughout his career he was responsible for the construction of well over one thousand. However, his proposal in 1830 for a suspension bridge to span the Avon Gorge at Bristol (see Plate 18, p52) could be classified as ugly in comparison to Brunel's design, and the reasons for this are discussed in Chapter 1.

Telford's involvement in bridge construction commenced in 1775, when as an apprentice to Andrew Thompson, a master mason, he worked on the construction of an elegant three-span masonry arch bridge crossing the River Esk at Langholm. He went on to build, over a period of nearly sixty years, numerous bridges of structural and

Plate 1 Designs by Telford for narrow lock gates (*from* Telford's Atlas, *Richard Packer*)

Timber Gates for Narrow Locks.

Lower
Upper

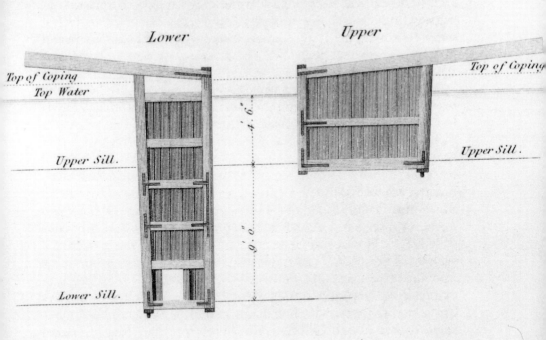

Top of Coping

Top Water

Upper Sill.

4' 6"

9' 0"

Top of Coping

Upper Sill.

Lower Sill.

Iron Gates for Narrow Locks.

Upper
Lower

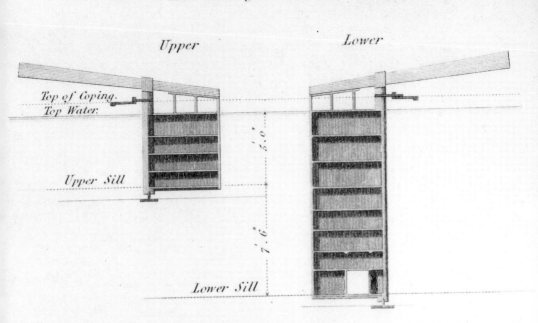

Top of Coping.

Top Water.

Upper Sill

5' 0"

7' 6"

Lower Sill

architectural merit, including the world's largest span: the Menai Suspension Bridge, opened in 1826 (see Plate 14, p46). In order to put Telford's contribution to the design and construction of bridges in context, it is necessary to trace their development up to the end of the eighteenth century.

The design of all bridges is based on one or more of three structural forms which were all developed from nature. In primitive times, travellers merely waded through shallow streams or leapt across a series of rock outcrops (stepping stones). In some cases, a fallen tree would conveniently span over rock outcrops or a stream to form a crude beam bridge, or a rock fall would provide a natural arch. In warmer climates, intertwined vines formed a natural suspension bridge. The date at which man-made forms of the beam, arch and chain were first built is a matter of speculation. Arch bridges have been recorded as far back as 4000 BC and it is probable that crude forms of beam bridge were developed even earlier. Prior to considering the development of bridge forms up to the eighteenth century, their structural action will be briefly explained in qualitative terms. With the notable exceptions of the Menai and Conwy suspension bridges (see Chapter 5) Telford made extensive use of the arch form, and a simple quantification of its struc-

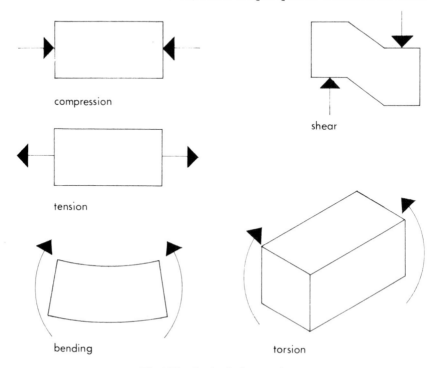

compression

shear

tension

bending

torsion

Fig 4 The five basic force actions

tural action is given in the Technical Appendix. In order to gain an appreciation of the structural action of a particular form of bridge, it is necessary to consider the loads acting on it. Essentially, the loads comprise the self or dead weight of the bridge, imposed loads arising from vehicles, pedestrians and so on, and those due to the elements, in particular wind action on suspension bridges. The force actions induced by the loadings are compression, tension, bending, shear and torsion, shown diagrammatically in Fig 4. Compression and tension induce shortening and extension of the material fibres respectively, and bending in the sense shown by the arrows causes the top fibres to be compressed and the bottom fibres to be extended. Thus bending induces both tension and compression. Shear is a measure of the tendency for racking or sliding of one part of the section relative to the adjacent part and torsion induces twisting of the cross section, both of which generate compression and tension. Thus it is possible to make a preliminary assessment of the structural potential of materials by considering their resistance to compression and tension. This is illustrated in Table 2 for a number of construction materials.

Table 2 Resistance of structural materials to force actions

| Material | Force action | | Approximate unit weight | |
	Compression	Tension	kN/m^3	lb/ft^3
Timber	●	●	5	33
Brick	●		19	125
Masonry	●		20	130
Concrete	●		24	155
Cast iron	●		78	500
Wrought iron	●	●	78	500

These materials were available to Telford and it will be noted that only two — timber and wrought iron — have a significant resistance to a tensile force action producing extension of the material fibres. Returning to the classical forms of bridge construction — beam, arch and suspension — the dominant force actions are illustrated in Fig 5. Thus it can be seen from Table 2 that for the materials largely used by Telford for bridge construction, the appropriate structural form is:

Masonry	Arch
Cast iron	Arch
Wrought iron	Suspension/beam

To return to the historical development of bridges, the first organised bridge building on a large scale took place during the expansion of the Roman Empire. The Romans built numerous bridges in masonry and

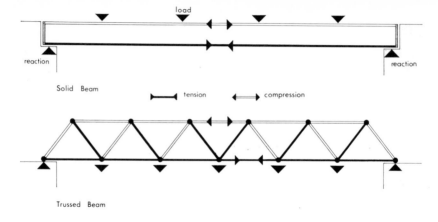

Fig 5a) The dominant force actions on a solid beam bridge and a trussed beam bridge

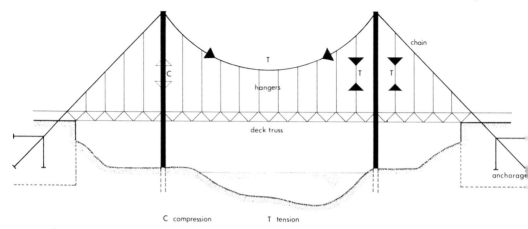

b) Suspension bridge

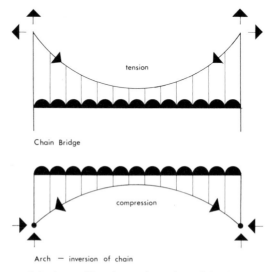

c) Arch considered as an inversion of the chain

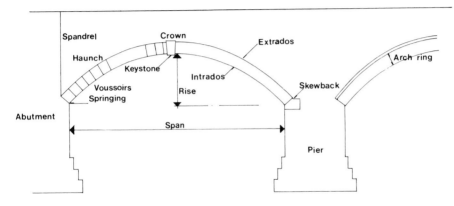

Fig 6 The components of the masonry arch

timber to carry roads and water (aqueducts). Although the Romans had no means of calculating their structures, they were excellent constructors and were able to direct large labour forces supervised by technicians. Telford had a similar ability, as will be demonstrated in subsequent chapters. The use of stone for beam bridges has obvious limitations, as its resistance to bending is low and the problems involved in cutting and transportation of large stone slabs are formidable. This can be overcome in arch construction by the use of wedge-shaped segments or voussoirs (see Fig 6), built up side by side on timber staging until the top stone (keystone) at the crown of the arch is pushed home. A wall (spandrel) is then built up to the road level. On removal of the staging, the loads induce compression in the voussoirs and the tendency for outward movement is contained by abutments (see Technical Appendix). The semicircular stone arch is characteristic of Roman bridge construction. Wedges, ramps or hoisting gear were employed to move the voussoirs into position on the temporary timber staging. The voussoirs were connected by mortar or iron clamps or sometimes dressed to fit.

With the decline of the Roman Empire, the art of bridge building in Europe fell into decay. Elsewhere, some remarkable bridges were built, in particular Chaochow Bridge in China, originally known as Anchi (safe crossing) Bridge. It was built between 605 and 617 over the Hsiacho River. In contrast to Roman semicircular arches, it was constructed in segmental form with a span of 123ft (37m) and a rise of 23ft (9.8m). To reduce the thrust on the abutments, the spandrels were pierced, which reduced the self-weight. The open spandrels also served to direct flood waters and reduce their impact on the bridge. It stands today and represents a significant technical advance over Roman arch construction.

In medieval times, extensive road and bridge works were carried out under the direction of the monasteries: the first stone bridge to be built across the Thames at London was begun in 1176 and the work was directed by a priest, Peter Colechurch. The structure consisted of 20 arches and was completed in 1209. Technical features of medieval bridges were the use of triangular projections from the pier, known as cutwaters, and the development of the ribbed arch. The cutwaters streamlined the flow of water round the piers and if taken up to the road level were used for pedestrians to shelter from passing carts and horsemen. The use of separate arch ribs, across which thinner stones could be laid, reduced the quantity of material required and thus the load on the foundations. The Renaissance saw the evolution of the scientific attitude to the design of structures: Leonardo da Vinci and Galileo Galilei made several important advances in the understanding of the strength of materials, though little notice was taken of their work at the time. Palladio, the famous Italian architect, worked on designs for timber truss bridges (see Fig 5) which were used for spans up to 100ft (31m). The arch bridge is most characteristic of Renaissance engineering skill, the segmental arch replacing the semicircular form used by the Romans.

During the eighteenth century, scientific attitudes were generally introduced into various fields of engineering. Mathematics and structural theory were rapidly developing and in 1747 the Ecole des Ponts et Chaussées was founded in Paris for training engineers in road and bridge works. At this time, France was ahead of other countries in the development of structural theory and the Ecole played an important part in the evolution of modern bridge engineering. The school's first director was Jean-Rodolphe Perronet (1707–94), one of the world's greatest designers of arch bridges. Two of his best works were the Pont Neuilly, crossing the Seine below Paris, and the Pont de la Concorde in Paris. The Neuilly Bridge had five arches of about 120ft (37m) span with a 30ft (9m) rise. The form of the arch used by Perronet in this bridge was copied by Telford in the design of Over Bridge, spanning the River Severn at Gloucester (see Chapter 2). Perronet appreciated that for a series of equal arch spans the thrusts at the intermediate piers of a multispan arch would be balanced for the dead load. Thus he adopted a small pier width to span ratio which increased the waterway opening and improved the appearance of his arches. This ratio for the Neuilly bridge was about 1:10. At this time, it was common practice to use a ratio of 1:5 while the Romans generally adopted a ratio of 1:3, each pier acting as an abutment so that if one span was destroyed, the others would not collapse.

In Britain there was little use of structural theory during the eighteenth century, and the most important development was the completion in 1780 of the cast-iron bridge spanning the River Severn at Coalbrookdale in Shropshire. This bridge is described in Chapter 2 and there is little doubt that it significantly influenced Telford's subsequent and brilliant exploitation of the use of cast iron for arch bridges. However, the stone arch remained the dominant form of construction in the eighteenth century, and at the time Telford was born William Edwards was struggling to complete a shallow masonry arch bridge over the River Taff at Pontypridd. Edwards used the technique of piercing the spandrels (as in Chaochow Bridge, China, known as the Great Stone Bridge) but it took several attempts to produce a stable structure.

There are records of suspension (chain) bridges in China and Kashmir built as early as the first century AD. The first recorded appearance in Europe was the publication of a drawing of a suspension bridge by Fausto Veranzio in 1595. It was not until the beginning of the nineteenth century that chain bridges capable of carrying vehicular traffic were developed. An American judge, James Finley, is generally recognised as being the pioneer of modern suspension bridge design, and he gives an interesting account of how they should be constructed (E. L. Kemp):

To find the proportions of the several parts of a Bridge of one hundred and fifty inches for the length of the bridge, draw a horizontal line between these two points representing the underside on the lower tiers of joists — on this line mark off spaces for the number of joists intended in the lower tier, and raise perpendiculars, twenty-three inches and one quarter above the horizontal line — the thread must be so slack that when loaded, the middle of it will sink to the horizontal line; then attach equal weights to the thread at each of the perpendiculars and mark carefully where the line intersects each of them.

As the bridge has no support but the chains, two things ought to be accurately understood; i.e., how much iron can bear at a direct pull endwise, and what it can bear in the other positions in which it is to be employed. As to the first, my experiments agree with the opinions of those who have investigated the subject; but I have made my calculations at 60 000lb to the inch square bar, which is something less than the strength of iron of the lowest quality.

But what a chain will bear when the two ends are fastened, and the weight affixed to the middle, or rather equally distributed along it, is a question that I presume may be determined by fastening one end of a line, and extending the other horizontally over a pully-whirl with a given weight attached to it (say 10lb), then let as many pounds be placed along the middle part at distances horizontally equal. The middle part of the line will then represent the chains loaded as when they support the bridge. The end that hangs in the manner of a plummet, determines the tension, and the pully-whirl equalizes it between the two parts.

This technique was adopted by Telford in the construction of the Menai Suspension Bridge (1818–26) (see Chapter 5).

Telford's bridge building career commenced five years before the completion of the world's first iron bridge and at a time when masonry arch bridges were reaching the peak of their technical development. Telford took little account of theory in his bridge designs but, as we shall see, made extensive use of testing the exploitation of the structural potential of cast and wrought iron. Hopefully, the following chapters will demonstrate the technical and aesthetic quality of Telford's bridge designs and his immense contribution to the art of bridge engineering.

Bridges are key elements in Britain's road network and many of Telford's bridges still contribute to the national stock of over 150,000 public road bridges. About 25 per cent of these bridges are of masonry or brick arch construction with an average span of about 35ft (10.5m) for spans in excess of 16ft (5m). This stock of arch bridges is a valuable national asset and it is fortunate that the masonry arch is the most durable form of bridge construction. However, many of these bridges are between 100 and 200 years old and the ravages of wind, rain and floods are beginning to take their toll. The Department of Transport, the Transport and Road Research Laboratory and County Councils are paying increasing attention to the assessment and maintenance of highway bridges. Over the past three decades, the intensity, number and weight of vehicles has increased significantly on all classes of road and this has exacerbated the problem of maintaining the integrity of ageing arch bridges. An example of recent repairs to one of Telford's more important Highland bridges, Lovat Bridge, which crosses the River Beauly in Inverness-shire, is described in Chapter 8. It is also referred to in the Gazetteer (p176).

Unfortunately, it is not just the older masonry and brick arch bridges that are in need of repair. Recently, attention has been focused on the lack of durability of a significant number of modern reinforced concrete bridges which represent over one-third of the national stock. The majority of concrete bridges are of beam form and contain embedded metal (reinforcement) to resist tension and control cracking. The composite material, reinforced concrete, suffers from the disadvantage that corrosion of the embedded metal leads to cracking and spalling of the concrete. Concrete without reinforcement is more suited to the arch form, and in the author's opinion greater attention should be paid to the potential of using concrete without reinforcement for arch bridges in which compression dominates. The durability of this form of construction is comparable with that of the masonry arch, the long-term stability of which has been adequately demonstrated in Telford's bridges.

CHRONICLE OF
PEOPLE AND EVENTS

c1200	Flash locks existed on River Thames
c1300–1400	Construction of canals running into the city of Milan. Use of crude locks consisting of a single gate being raised and lowered
1452	Leonardo da Vinci born, artist, scientist and engineer (d1519)
c1500	Drawing by Leonardo da Vinci of a lock with mitred gates at San Marco
c1550	Coaches first used on English roads
c1550	Mitre-gate pound locks introduced in France
1555	The first Highway Act passed dealing with the upkeep of roads
1567	First pound locks in England on Exeter Canal
1635	Completion of three locks on River Thames at Iffley, Sandford and Abingdon
1650	London to Edinburgh coach service started
1653	Opening of Wey Navigation, 15 miles Weybridge to Guildford. Engineer Sir Richard Western (1591–1652)
1653	The first Turnpike Act passed required travellers to pay a toll in return for the use of roads
1703	Aire and Calder Navigation opened, 42 miles Weeland to Leeds and Wakefield, engineer John Hadley
1716	James Brindley born, canal engineer (d1772)
1717	John Metcalf born, road maker (d1810)
c1720	Several thousand toll gates (turnpikes) in use in Britain
1724	John Smeaton born, engineer (d1792)
1724	John Telford born, the Unblameable Shepherd (d1757)
1736	Duke of Bridgewater born (d1803)
1736	James Watt born, engineer (d1819)
1737	General George Wade (1673–1748) had completed 250 miles of road in Scotland

1745	William Jessop born, canal engineer (d1814)
1747	Ecole des Ponts et Chaussées founded in Paris for training engineers in construction work on highways, tunnels and bridges. First director Jean Rodolphe Perronet (1708–94)
1757	Completion of the Sankey Canel, the earliest canal of the Industrial Revolution, 10 miles St Helens coalfield to the Mersey, engineer Henry Berry (1720–1812)
1757	John Telford died (November). Memorial in disused graveyard at Westerkirk (Bentpath)
1757	Thomas Telford born (9 August), engineer
1761	John Rennie born, engineer (d1824)
1764	Completion of Calder Navigation, 24 miles Wakefield to Halifax, engineer John Smeaton
1769	Marc Isambard Brunel born (25 April), engineer (d1849)
1771	Society of Civil Engineers founded by John Smeaton and other practising engineers who had already gained extensive experience
1774	Robert Southey born, poet and friend of Thomas Telford (d1843)
1775	Thomas Telford worked with Andrew Thompson on Langholm Bridge, Eskdale
1777	Completion of the Trent and Mersey Canal, 93½ miles from River Trent at Shardlow to Runcorn Gap with 75 locks and 5 tunnels, engineers James Brindley and Hugh Henshall
1779–80	Completion of Iron Bridge at Coalbrookdale over River Severn
1780	Thomas Telford left Eskdale to work as a stonemason in Edinburgh
1781	George Stephenson born (9 June), engineer (d1848)
1782	Thomas Telford employed as a stonemason on Somerset House
1784	Thomas Telford appointed building superintendent for the new Commissioner's House at Portsmouth Naval Dockyard
1788	Thomas Telford appointed surveyor of public works for the County of Shropshire
1792	Completion of Montford Bridge, River Severn, Shropshire, A5(T)

1796	Opening of Buildwas Bridge, River Severn, Shropshire (replaced 1905)
1796	Opening of Longdon on Tern Aqueduct, Shrewsbury Canal, Shropshire
1798	Completion of Bewdley Bridge, River Severn, Worcestershire
1801	Completion of Chirk Aqueduct over River Ceiriog, Ellesmere Canal
1803	Robert Stephenson born, (16 October) engineer (d1859)
1805	Grand Junction Canal, 93½ miles opened from Oxford Canal to River Thames at Brentford including Blisworth Tunnel, chief engineer William Jessop
1805	Opening of Pont Cysyllte Aqueduct, River Dee near Llangollen, Ellesmere Canal
1806	Isambard Kingdom Brunel born (9 April), engineer (d1859)
1808	Opening of Dunkeld Bridge over River Tay, Perthshire
1810	Thomas Telford's first report on the Holyhead Road
1812	Opening of Bonar Bridge, Dornoch Firth (destroyed c1890)
1814	Opening of Lovat (Beauly) Bridge over the River Beauly, near Inverness
1815	Opening of Craigellachie Bridge, River Spey
1816	Opening of Waterloo Bridge, River Conwy, Betws-y-Coed (bears date 1815)
1817	Exchequer Loan Commission created to assist financing suitable public works
1818	Inaugural meeting of the Institution of Civil Engineers (2 January) founded by a group of young engineers
1820	Regent's Canal opened to link Paddington arm of Grand Junction Canal with London's docks
1820	Thomas Telford became first president of the Institution of Civil Engineers, presidential address 21 March 1820
1822	Caledonian Canal opened for first through passage by Steam Yacht & Sloop *Caledonia* (23 October)
1822	Opening of Cartland Crags Bridge over Mouse Water, near Lanark
1825	Opening of Over Bridge, River Severn, Gloucester

1825	Opening of Stockton & Darlington Railway (27 September), engineers George and Robert Stephenson
1826	Conwy Suspension Bridge opened (summer)
1826	Menai Suspension Bridge opened for public traffic (Monday 30 January)
1826	Opening of Holt Fleet Bridge, River Severn, Worcestershire
1826	Opening of Mythe Bridge, River Severn, Tewkesbury
1827	Opening of Harecastle Tunnel (Trent and Mersey Canal). Telford's tunnel built parallel to Brindley's tunnel (1792)
1828	The first ship entered St Katharine Docks (25 October)
1829	Opening of Galton Bridge, Birmingham Canal, Smethwick
1830	Formal opening of the Liverpool & Manchester Railway (15 September), engineers George and Robert Stephenson
1831	Opening of Dean Bridge, Water of Leith, Edinburgh
1832	Formal opening of the Gotha Canal, Sweden (26 September)
1834	Thomas Telford died (22 September) buried in the nave of Westminster Abbey
1835	Opening of the Birmingham and Liverpool Junction Canal (March) for through passage (single boat) over Shelmore Great Bank
1836	First volume of transactions of the Institution of Civil Engineers published by John Weale with autographs of eminent engineers including Thomas Telford

Some influential names in the life of Thomas Telford

John Telford	Shepherd, father of Thomas Telford
Janet Telford	Wife of John Telford (maiden name Janet Jackson)
William Little	School friend of Thomas Telford, brother of Andrew
Andrew Little	School friend of Thomas Telford, surgeon, blinded at sea
Matthew Davidson	Friend of Thomas Telford, stonemason
Sir James Johnstone	Landowner in Eskdale
Thomas Jackson	Land steward of the Johnstones, nephew of Janet Jackson
Andrew Thompson	Master mason in Langholm
Miss Pasley	Langholm, encouraged Thomas Telford in his literary pursuits
John Pasley	Brother of Miss Pasley, London merchant
Robert Adam	Architect
Sir William Chambers	Architect
William Johnstone	Youngest brother of Sir James Johnstone, married Miss Pulteney, changed his name to Pulteney. Became MP for Shrewsbury and a wealthy landowner
John Simpson	Mason from Shrewsbury
William Hazledine	Iron founder. Ironworks at Plas Kynaston and Shrewsbury
William Stuttle	William Hazledine's foreman
John Wilson	Stonemason
John Mitchell	Stonemason, subsequently superintendent of Highland roads
John Rickman	Friend of Thomas Telford and Secretary of the Caledonian Canal and Highland Roads and Bridges Commissions
Robert Southey	Poet Laureate and friend of Thomas Telford
William Purvis	Engineering assistant to Thomas Telford
John Gibb	Engineering assistant to Thomas Telford

1
THOMAS TELFORD (1757–1834): HIS LIFE AND WORK

I admire commercial enterprise, it is the vigorous outgrowth of our in-dustrial life: I admire everything that gives it free scope, as, wherever it goes, activity, energy, intelligence — all that we call civilisation — accompany it; but I hold that the aim and end of all ought not to be a mere bag of money, but something far higher and far better.

(THOMAS TELFORD)

At the end of September 1985, the author embarked on a tedious 320 mile (515km) journey from London to Eskdale to visit the scene of Thomas Telford's early life. The boredom of the seven-hour haul along the M1, M6 and A7 was quickly relieved about 20 miles (32km) north of Carlisle on approaching the 'Muckle Toon' of Langholm.

The approaches to Langholm and Eskdale are marked by the 100ft (30.5m) high monument erected on White Hill to honour General Sir John Malcolm, soldier, diplomat, scholar and writer, one of a number of distinguished names, including Telford's, associated with Lang-holm. A statue of Sir John's brother, Admiral Sir Malcolm Pulteney, stands in Langholm Library Garden. The name Pulteney has strong connections with the development of Telford's civil engineering career.

The town of Langholm, situated amidst the hills and woods and streams of Eskdale, has numerous associations with Telford, including an elegant stone arch bridge which crosses the cool bustling waters of the River Esk. To reach Telford's birthplace, it is necessary to cross this bridge into the inevitable 'Telford Road' and then along the B709 (see Gazetteer, p172) to the village of Bentpath. On crossing the Esk, with Westerkirk Church to be seen on the right, a road follows the course of the Esk and then one of its tributaries, Meggat Water.

It is easy to appreciate the ageing Telford writing in his autobiography, 'I still recollect with pride and pleasure my native parish of Westerkirk, on the banks of the Esk, where I was born'.

Thomas Telford was born on 9 August 1757 at Glendinning on the banks of Meggat Water. His father, John Telford, died a few months later. A memorial to John Telford, inscribed by his son, is to be found in a disused graveyard up the hill from Westerkirk Church, Bentpath (Plate 2).

> In Memory of John Telford who, after living 33 years an
> Unblameable Shepherd, Died at Glendinning, November, 1757.

The young Telford and his mother Janet moved to Crooks Cottage, about halfway between Bentpath and Glendinning. Plate 3 shows the road leading from Bentpath to Glendinning.

Telford attended the local parish school at Westerkirk and became acquainted with the brothers William and Andrew Little. This was to develop into a close friendship and extracts from Telford's letters to Andrew Little are quoted later. Following ill-treatment by a stonemason at Lochmaben, Telford was apprenticed to Andrew Thompson, a master mason. Amongst other work, he assisted Thompson in the construction of the stone arch bridge over the Esk at Langholm, mentioned previously. This was an admirable apprenticeship for a career involving the construction of hundreds of arch bridges. It was complemented by a desire for learning — 'knowledge is my most ardent pursuit' — and an interest in poetry. He wrote of Eskdale in 1784:

> Deep 'mid the green sequester'd glens below
> Where murmuring streams among the alders flow
> Where flowery meadows down their margins spread
> And the brown hamlet lifts its humble head
> There, round his little fields, the peasant strays
> And sees his flock along the mountain graze.

While not the work of a great poet, the verse demonstrates Telford's love of Eskdale. In the pursuit of knowledge, Telford was assisted by an elderly lady, Miss Pasley, who gave him access to her bookshelves.

In addition to the Esk Bridge, on the western abutment of which is to be found his mason's mark, there are a number of other examples of Telford's craftsmanship in Langholm, including a doorway adjacent to the library.

By 1780, the work in Langholm was not sufficient to occupy Telford's fertile mind and he left Eskdale and 'studied all that was to be seen in Edinburgh'. He returned to Eskdale for a fleeting visit: 'Having acquired the rudiments of my profession, I considered that my native country afforded few opportunities of exercising it to any extent, and therefore judged it advisable (like many of my countrymen) to proceed southwards, where industry might find more employment and be better remunerated'. Telford's wages in Langholm were eighteen pence a day.

At the end of January 1782, armed with his mallet and chisels and a letter of introduction from Miss Pasley to her brother, John, Telford set

Plate 2 *(inset)* Memorial stone to John Telford in Westerkirk
Church graveyard, Bentpath, 'In Memory of John Telford who,
after living 33 years an Unblameable Shepherd . . .' *(Derrick Beckett)*

Plate 3 The road leading from Bentpath to Glendinning,
Crooks on the left, looking down towards the River Esk
(Derrick Beckett)

off for '. . . The great world of London'. He was able to make the journey by horse as, fortuitously, Sir James Johnstone, a wealthy landowner, wished to deliver a horse to a relative in London.

Through John Pasley, Telford was introduced to two eminent architects, Robert Adam and Sir William Chambers. He was employed by Sir William Chambers to work on Somerset House. In later years, Telford was walking over Waterloo Bridge with a friend and pointed to some stonework on the south-west corner of Somerset House: 'You see those stones there: forty years since I hewed and laid them, when working on that building as a common mason' (Plate 4).

Within two decades, the common mason was to become an eminent architect and engineer assisted by the patronage of William Johnstone, the younger brother of Sir James Johnstone. William Johnstone was fortunate in marrying Miss Pulteney, niece of the Earl of Bath. Johnstone changed his name to Pulteney, inherited several large estates and became Member of Parliament for Shrewsbury. Through Pulteney, Telford obtained a number of commissions (work on Somerset House was slowing down) including Sir James Johnstone's home in Eskdale.

Plate 4 Telford worked as a stonemason on the south-west corner of Somerset House between 1782 and 1784 *(Derrick Beckett)*

In 1784, Telford was appointed to superintend the construction of the Commissioner's house and other buildings at Portsmouth Dockyard (see Plate 5). On 1 February 1786 he wrote to Andrew Little (S. Smiles):

I rise in the morning at 7 (February 1st), and will get up earlier as the days lengthen until it come to 5 o'clock. I immediately set to work to make out accounts, write on matters of business, or draw, until breakfast, which is at 9. Then I go into the Yard about 10, see that all are at their posts, and am ready to advise about any matters that may require attention. This, and going round the several works, occupies until about dinner-time, which is at 2; and after that I again go round and attend to what may be wanted. I draw till 5; then tea; and after that I write, draw, or read until half after 9; then comes supper and bed. This is my ordinary round, unless when I dine or spend an evening with a friend; but I do not make many friends, being very particular, nay, nice to a degree. My business requires a great deal of writing and drawing, and this work I always take care to keep under by reserving my time for it, and being in advance of my work rather than behind it. Then, as knowledge is my most ardent pursuit, a thousand things occur which call for investigation which would pass unnoticed by those who are content to trudge only in the beaten path. I am not contented unless I can give a reason for every particular method or practice which is pursued. Hence I am now very deep in chemistry. The mode of making mortar in the best way led me to inquire into the nature of lime. Having, in pursuit of this inquiry, looked into some books on chemistry, I perceived the field was boundless; but that to assign satisfactory reasons for many mechanical processes required a general knowledge of that science. I have therefore borrowed a MS. copy of Dr. Black's Lectures. I have bought his 'Experiments on Magnesia and Quicklime', and also Fourcroy's Lectures, translated from the French by one Mr. Elliot, of Edinburgh. And I am determined to study the subject with unwearied attention until I attain some accurate knowledge of chemistry, which is of no less use in the practice of the arts than it is in that of medicine.

This letter gives a most revealing insight into Telford's life and character and he also recalled that he has his hair powdered twice a day, and puts on a clean shirt three times a week. The work at Portsmouth

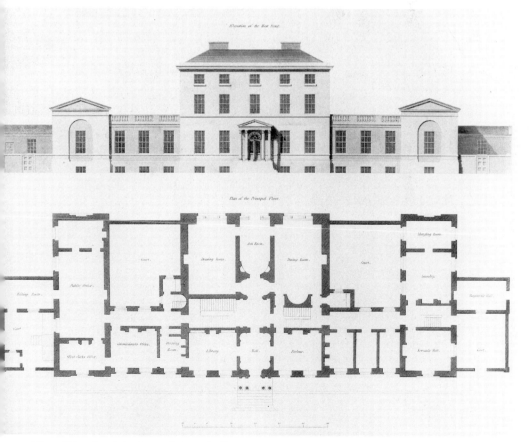

Plate 5 Details of the Commissioner's House at Portsmouth Dockyard (*from* Telford's Atlas, *Richard Packer*)

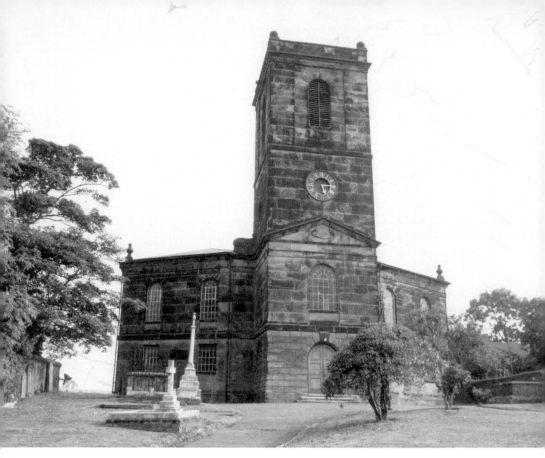

Plate 6 Telford designed a number of churches, including St Michael's, Madeley (1793) (*Derrick Beckett*)

Plate 7 One of a number of bridges built by Telford over the River Severn, Montford Bridge, completed in 1792, still carries the heavily-trafficked London to Holyhead Road A5(T) (*Derrick Beckett*)

was completed at the end of 1786 and he was invited by William Pulteney to work on the restoration of Shrewsbury Castle.

In the period 1786 to 1793, Telford's work in the Shrewsbury area was essentially that of an architect — he referred to it as architectural odd-jobbery (J. B. Lawson). He made a telling remark about contemporary architects '. . . blundering round about a meaning' (L. T. C. Rolt). However, his architectural achievements were considerable, and in addition to working on Shrewsbury Castle and the new gaol, Telford designed a number of churches, including St Michael's, Madeley (1793) (see Plate 6). Three appointments led to an illustrious career in civil engineering and his achievements merit at least equal ranking with those of the great railway engineers, Robert Stephenson (1803–59) and current hero of nineteenth-century engineering achievements, Isambard Kingdom Brunel (1806–59). These appointments were:

1788   Surveyor to the County of Shropshire
1793   General agent, surveyor, engineer, architect and overlooker of the works for the Ellesmere Canal (C. Hadfield and A. W. Skempton)
1795   Engineer to the Shrewsbury Canal following the death of Josiah Clawes.

As Surveyor to the County of Shropshire, Telford designed the first of a number of major bridges over the River Severn: Montford Bridge (Plate 7). It was constructed between 1790 and 1792 and is described in Chapter 2.

Work on the Ellesmere Canal brought Telford into contact with William Jessop (1745–1814) with whom Telford worked on a number of major civil engineering projects over a period of twenty years. These included the Pont Cysyllte Aqueduct on the Ellesmere Canal (Chapter 3) and the Caledonian Canal (Chapter 7).

The purpose of Shrewsbury Canal was to link the East Shropshire coalfield with Shrewsbury and an Act for its construction was obtained in 1793 (A. R. K. Clayton). Josiah Clawes acted as engineer for about a year, and following his death at the end of 1794 he was succeeded by Telford. Much of the construction work had been completed by this time with the exception of the aqueduct at Longdon on Tern, which now stands in splendid isolation in the middle of a field (see Gazetteer, p159). In March 1795, Telford wrote to Andrew Little, 'I have just recommended an Iron Aqueduct for the most considerable; it is approved and will be executed under my direction upon a principle entirely new, and which I am endeavouring to establish with regard to the application of iron'.

Telford's pioneering work on the use of cast iron for the aqueduct at Longdon was of fundamental importance and he was subsequently able to utilise its potential to great effect on numerous structures which are described in later chapters.

A partly built stone aqueduct, designed by Clawes, was swept away by floods, leaving a sandstone abutment. Telford's design consisted of cast-iron trough sections supported by vertical and diagonal struts, and the trough was connected to the original abutment (see Plate 8). The trough, 186ft (57m) long, is made up of cast-iron sections bolted together (Plate 9). It can be seen that the footway is outside the trough (see Pont Cysyllte Aqueduct, p160). The ironwork was cast at William Reynolds' Ketley works and it was here that the cruciform section struts were subjected to extensive tests. The aqueduct was opened in March 1796. Plate 10 shows the detail at the base of the struts.

Plates 8–10 Longdon on Tern Aqueduct. The cast-iron trough is supported by vertical and diagonal cruciform struts. Note the original aqueduct on the right (*Derrick Beckett*)

(*inset*) The cast-iron trough with the footpath outside at Longdon on Tern, in contrast to Pont Cysyllte Aqueduct (see Plate 11) (*Derrick Beckett*) and the detail at the base of the cruciform struts of Longdon on Tern Aqueduct (*Derrick Beckett*)

45 feet

Plate 11 The arch ribs of Pont Cysyllte Aqueduct, which support the trough above, have a clear span of 45ft (13.8m) (*from* Telford's Atlas, *Richard Packer*)

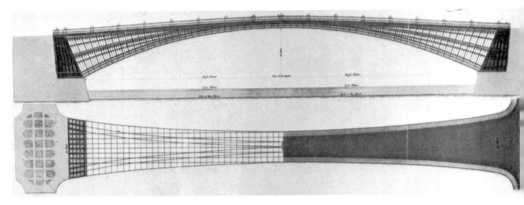

Fig 7 An illustration of Telford's proposal for a 600ft (183m) span cast-iron arch to bridge the Thames at London

In addition to the 1,007ft (308m) long Pont Cysyllte Aqueduct built between 1795 and 1805 to carry the Ellesmere Canal over the River Dee near Llangollen, Telford went even further to demonstrate his confidence in the use of cast iron. Although the Pont Cysyllte Aqueduct is a massive structure by any standards, the arch ribs are of relatively short span: 45ft (13.8m) between the stone piers (Plate 11). This span pales into insignificance compared with Telford's proposal in 1800 to bridge the Thames at London with a single cast-iron arch of 600ft (183m) span. The form of the bridge is shown in Fig 7 and if built would have been easily the largest span in the world. He subsequently built the world's largest span: the Menai Suspension Bridge, 579ft (177m), completed in 1826 (see Chapter 5). Unfortunately, the bridge was not built, possibly for economic reasons and lack of confidence in its technical feasibility. Technical aspects of Telford's proposals for a new London Bridge are discussed in the Technical Appendix.

Between 1800 and 1826, Telford was involved in a number of massive government-financed civil engineering projects. Through his association with William Pulteney, he advised the British Fisheries Society and this led to surveys of the Highlands and subsequent construction work on the Caledonian Canal (Chapter 7) and a network of roads and bridges in Scotland (Chapter 8). His work in Scotland also involved advising on harbour improvements, a major example being Aberdeen harbour. The original 1,200ft (367m) long pier designed in 1773 by the eminent civil engineer John Smeaton (1724–92) was extended by Telford and Jessop a further 800ft (245m) between 1810 and 1816. Details of the construction technique involved are shown in Plates 12 and 13, taken from *Telford's Atlas*.

A contemporary account of Telford's work in Scotland can be found in Robert Southev's *Journal of a Tour in Scotland in 1819*. The manu-

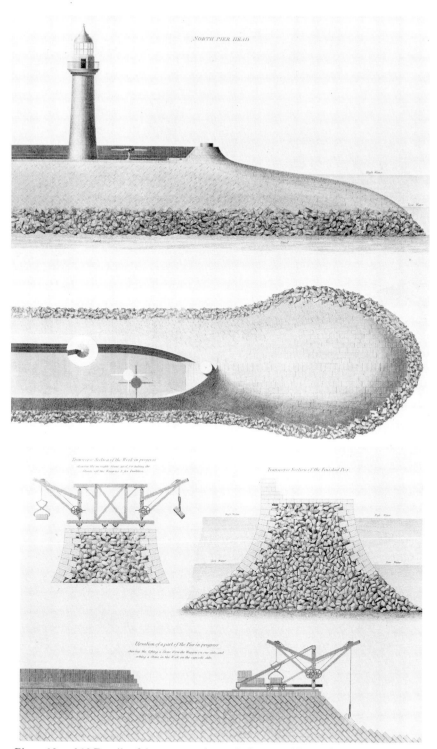

Plates 12 and 13 Details of the construction technique used by Telford and Jessop in the extension of the pier at Aberdeen harbour (*from* Telford's Atlas, *Richard Packer*)

script of the *Journal* was presented to the Library of the Institution of Civil Engineers in 1885 and reprinted by John Murray in 1928 to celebrate the 100th anniversary of the grant of a Royal Charter to the Institution. The tour was probably arranged by John Rickman, Telford's geographer, one of his executors and secretary to the Commissioners of the Caledonian Canal. Rickman was a friend of Southey and the party included Southey, Telford, Rickman, his wife and two children. The route was dictated by Telford's professional duties and commenced at Edinburgh on 17 August and was completed on 1 October. A friendly association between Robert Southey, the Poet Laureate, educated at Westminster and Balliol, and Thomas Telford, a stonemason from Eskdale, would seem unlikely, but Southey declared he was on cordial terms with Telford within five minutes of meeting him: 'There is so much intelligence in his countenance, so much frankness, kindness and hilarity about him, flowing from the never-failing wellspring of a happy nature'. By 23 August, the party had reached Dunkeld and Southey referred to Telford's bridge (see Chapter 8) as one of the finest in Scotland. Telford's work at Dundee harbour was inspected on 25 August: 'Telford's is a happy life: everywhere making roads, building bridges, forming canals and creating harbours — works of sure, solid, permanent utility; everywhere employing a great number of persons, selecting the most meritorious, and putting them forward in the world, in his own way'.

Aberdeen harbour was inspected on 28 August, including the pier described previously. This was followed by inspection of the harbour works at Banff and Cullen and the cast-iron bridge at Craigellachie was reached on 1 September: '. . . the bridge is of iron, beautifully light, in a situation where the utility of lightness is instantly perceived'.

During the following three weeks the party made a number of visits to the works on the Caledonian Canal between Inverness and Fort William. The return journey via Glasgow to Carlisle was completed by 1 October and 'Mr T' left to take the mail to Edinburgh.

In addition to describing Telford's engineering works, Southey's *Journal* gives many humorous accounts of hotel life: '. . . this is the only inn in which we have met with dishonesty in wine, Cape having been produced here for sherry; but the Port as it is everywhere, is good. Everywhere else we have had cream; here they say it is never to be had . . . In the poorer inns the sheets are generally calico; and in most places the towels are pieces of thin calico, hardly larger than doylies'.

About five years after the commencement of work on the Caledonian Canal, Telford was consulted by Admiral Count von Platen, with regard to the construction of a canal between Lake Vanern and the

North Sea

Baltic Sea

Fig 8 The route of the Gota Canal. Telford was consulted by Admiral Count von Platen
with regard to the construction of a canal between Lake Vanern and the Baltic

Baltic. A river and canal link (Trollhatte Canal) between the North
Sea at Goteborg and Lake Vanern was opened in 1800. Von Platen
wished to extend the work to form a navigable link between the
North Sea and the Baltic. Gota Canal completed this link (see Fig 8),
and is similar to the Caledonian Canal, consisting of natural and man-
made waterways. Telford visited Sweden twice in 1808 and with the
help of two assistants carried out a survey, prepared detailed plans and
submitted his report. The report was accepted and the work proceeded
with Telford making one more visit in 1813. The canal was not opened
until 1832, three years after Von Platen's death.

A further major government-financed project came Telford's way,
when in 1810 a Parliamentary Committee was set up to investigate the
state of the London and Holyhead Road (see Chapter 4). Telford was
commissioned to prepare a report and although it was extremely critical
of travelling conditions, it was not until 1815 that improvement works
commenced following the setting up of the Holyhead Road Commission. The improvements included the construction of the Menai
Suspension Bridge (see Plate 14), arguably the most impressive of all
Telford's contributions to civil engineering; its evolution, design and
construction are the subject of Chapter 5.

It is difficult to conceive that Telford could undertake further respon-
sibilities in a period which involved journeys from his London base to
North Wales and the North of Scotland and the preparation of numerous plans and reports, the construction of hundreds of miles of road and
major bridges (see the Chronicle of People and Events). Following the
Battle of Waterloo in 1815, England was in an economic depression
and, as a means of boosting trade and reducing unemployment, the Exchequer Bill Loan Commission was formed in 1817. Its purpose was to
assess the suitability of proposals for public works for financial aid and
Telford was appointed by the commissioners to advise on all works re-
quiring civil engineering expertise. Typical examples of the projects

Plate 14 The Menai Suspension Bridge when opened in 1826 was the world's largest, with a span of 579ft (177m) between the masonry towers (*Frances Gibson Smith*)

Plate 15 Kingston upon Thames Bridge (1828 and extensively rebuilt 1929) is typical of numerous projects in which Telford was involved through his role as technical adviser to the Exchequer Bill Loan Commission (*Derrick Beckett*)

which sought financial advice (A. Gibb) are Kingston Bridge (£40,000) and the Liverpool & Manchester Railway (£100,000). In 1828 the Corporation of Kingston upon Thames replaced the old wooden bridge with a multi-span stone arch (see Plate 15). It was widened in 1929 and extensively rebuilt.

The assistance to the Liverpool & Manchester Railway involved Telford meeting George Stephenson (1781–1848) and his criticism of Stephenson's organisation of the works (see Chapter 9).

In addition to his work on the Ellesmere and Shrewsbury canals, referred to previously, Telford was involved with a further 30 or more canal projects, four important examples being the Trent and Mersey Canal (Grand Trunk Canal), the Grand Junction Canal, the Birmingham Canal Navigation and the Birmingham and Liverpool Junction Canal (Shropshire Union). The Trent and Mersey Canal Act was passed in 1766 and James Brindley (1716–72) was appointed engineer. The canal, running 93½ miles (150km) between Derwent Mouth near Long Eaton and Preston Brook close to the Bridgewater Canal (see Introduction), took eleven years to build and involved the construction of Harecastle Tunnel at Kidsgrove. It was the largest tunnel of its day, 1¾ miles

(2.82km), but the cross section was so small, 9¼ft (2.83m) wide and 12ft (3.7m) high, that it was not possible to provide a towpath. The boats had to be 'legged' through the tunnel by men lying on the cabin roof and propelling the boat by 'walking' along the tunnel roof. Meanwhile, the horses were walked over Harecastle Hill. It could take three hours to leg through the tunnel, a hazardous experience as there were frequent roof falls. Increasing canal traffic made the tunnel a major bottleneck and further it was slowly sinking. In 1822, Telford advised the canal company to construct a second tunnel parallel to the first, but with a towpath (see Plate 16). It was built between 1824 and 1827 at a cost of £112,681, see detailed statement below (British Waterways Board):

Original building cost — Telford's Harecastle Tunnel

Detailed statement of expense incurred in forming Harecastle new tunnel.

	£
Fifteen shafts 9ft diameter	1,610
Driving heading through hill	7,057
Driving cross headings to carry off water	470
Driving heading in coal measures to drain the sand at north end of tunnel	540
Excavating the body of the tunnel and turning brickwork including timber, length 2926½ yards	43,435
Expense of towing path	9,600
Length of railway 6½ miles	7,000
Length providing bricks and mortar and centering	22,750
Labour on mortar and centering	1,537
Carriage of materials	4,060
Expense of open cutting, entrances and turnover bridges at each end of tunnel, erecting workshops, mortar mills, clay mills, engine houses, pumping water, damages of land, fence, agencies etc.	14,622
	£112,681

Total number of bricks on tunnel and works 8,814,681

Signed JAMES POTTER OF BRINKLOW
25-2-1833

With the construction of the second tunnel two-way working was possible but further subsidence led to the closure of Brindley's tunnel in 1918. By 1910 (British Waterways Board) the water level in two sections of Telford's tunnel was 13in (325mm) above the towpath level and a tug service was started in 1914. The tugs were electrically powered and the service operated until 1954. With the introduction of diesel/petrol pow-

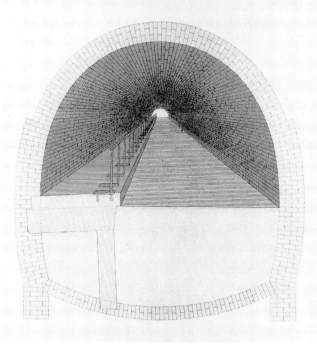

Cross Section of Tunnel

Plate 16 Telford's design for the second Harecastle Tunnel, built between 1824 and 1827 at a cost of £112,681. Note the towpath (*from* Telford's Atlas, *Richard Packer*)

ered craft which could pass through the tunnel under their own power, a further problem arose, that is, the extraction of foul air. A fan house was constructed at the south end between 1953 and 1954. Continuing general movement, leaks and deterioration of the original tunnel lining have over the years necessitated constant repairs and regular inspections are still required to monitor movement. By the time Telford's tunnel at Harecastle was completed, he had reached the age of 70. Although his health was declining by 1827, work on Harecastle Tunnel coincided with another major project which was in hand at London: St Katharine Docks. The docks were opened in October 1828 and their construction is described in Chapter 6.

Returning to the second of the four major canal projects listed previously, the Act for the construction of the Grand Junction Canal was given assent by George III 27 years after that for the Grand Trunk Canal. The route was from the Oxford Canal at Braunston (opened in 1778) in Northamptonshire through Buckinghamshire and Hertfordshire to the Thames at Brentford, Middlesex. Work commenced in 1793 on the construction of the 93½ mile (150km) route with William

Jessop as chief engineer. It involved the construction of 100 locks and two major tunnels: at Braunston 6,146ft (1,873m) and Blisworth 9,227ft (2,812m). The work, with the exception of Blisworth Tunnel, was completed in late 1800. Blisworth Tunnel was cut from nineteen vertical shafts and opened in 1805. The branch to Paddington was completed in the period 1795 to 1801, followed by Regent's Canal, 1812–20, thus forming a direct link to London's docks. Telford's involvement commenced in 1805 when he was asked to prepare an independent report and subsequently advised on a number of matters. Through Telford's appointment as technical adviser to the Exchequer Bill Loan Commission, Regent's Canal (running from the Grand Junction Canal at Paddington, by Regent's Park and Islington to the Thames at Limehouse) received a series of loans totalling £250,000.

The Birmingham Canal Navigations are a complex network of waterways which were built to link the industrial areas round Birmingham with other main canals and the rivers Trent, Mersey, Thames and Severn. The network was developed by a number of rival companies and an Act for the construction of the first section was obtained in 1768. The route was surveyed by Brindley and it was built to link Aldersley on the line of the proposed Staffordshire and Worcestershire Canal and the centre of Birmingham. The engineer chose a winding, 22½ mile (36km) route to avoid major engineering works and it was opened in 1772. It was a commercial success and traffic increased to a level at which it was necessary to carry out improvements. The summit at Smethwick was lowered in the 1790s, which reduced the number of locks by six. But this was not enough to cope with the continuing traffic increase and in 1825 Telford was appointed to investigate means of improving the route of the canal. Telford's proposals for improving the 'Old' Main Line, as it was called, were accepted and work on the 'New' Main Line continued until several years after his death. The distance from Birmingham to Aldersley was reduced by 7 miles (11km) by constructing a straight canal through Smethwick with massive cuttings and embankments. The New Line was 40ft (12m) wide with a double towpath which is clearly seen in Plate 17. It also shows the last of Telford's major cast-iron bridges, which was built in 1829 with the ironwork supplied by the Horseley Company. As with other Telford designs, the span is 150ft (46m) over the cutting. The distance between the roadway and the canal is 70ft (21m), which indicates the massive excavation required to form the cutting. The bridge is now closed to vehicular traffic.

At the time of the completion of Galton Bridge, an advertisement appeared in a number of newspapers inviting designs for the erection of a suspension bridge at Clifton Down over the River Avon, Bristol. The

Plate 17 Telford's 'New' Main Line passed through Smethwick in a massive cutting. The last of Telford's major cast-iron bridges, Galton Bridge, 150ft (46m) span, was built in 1829 *(Derrick Beckett)*

response was considerable and in all 22 designs were submitted, including four by the 23 year old Isambard Kingdom Brunel (1806–59). Brunel had spent two days studying Telford's Menai Bridge before submitting his designs with spans varying from 720ft (220m) to over 1,000ft (306m). The Bridge Committee called in Telford for an expert opinion. He reported that all the designs were unsatisfactory and the Bridge Committee invited him to submit his own design, which consisted of massive Gothic-style piers rising from the bottom of the Avon Gorge to support a three-span suspended deck (Plate 18).

Telford was concerned about the movement of the deck of the Menai Bridge and this possibly, coupled with the conservatism of old age, led to his opinion that the maximum admissible span for a suspension bridge was 600ft (183m), slightly greater than the Menai. Public opinion was against Telford's proposal and Brunel commented: 'As the distance between the opposite rocks was considerably less than what had always been considered as the limits to which suspension bridges might be carried, the idea of going to the bottom of such a valley for the purpose of raising at great expense two intermediate supports hardly occurred to me' — a damning comment by the 23 year old Brunel on the work of the country's most eminent civil engineer.

It is difficult to imagine a more romantic setting for a bridge than the Avon Gorge and Telford's design certainly did not complement its

Plate 18 The designs by Brunel and Telford for the Clifton Bridge at Bristol

natural beauty. Fortunately, the Committee decided to announce a second competition and Telford's and Brunel's designs were amongst the five short-listed. Davies Gilbert (1767–1839), president of the Royal Society, was appointed to assess the designs — a wise choice as Gilbert (in 1817 he changed his name from Giddy to Gilbert) had previously advised on the Menai Bridge and made an important contribution to the theory of suspension bridges. Brunel's design satisfied the requirement that the stress in the chains should not exceed 5.5 tons/in^2 (85 N/mm^2) and on the 26 March 1831 he was formally appointed to design and construct the bridge. It was not completed until five years after Brunel's death and Brunel's original proposals for the chains and deck were extensively modified. To put the matter in context, if the bridge had been built to Brunel's original specifications, it would have suffered from the same problems with deck movement as the Menai Bridge.

Two major civil engineering works which were to occupy Telford until his death in September 1834 were the Birmingham and Liverpool Junction Canal, which now forms part of the Shropshire Union Canal (see Fig 9). and the Fens drainage schemes. The Shropshire Union Canal consists of four sections which were amalgamated in 1845:

(i)   The Chester Canal from Chester to Nantwich, opened in 1779.

(ii)   The Wirral Line of the Ellesmere Canal from Ellesmere Port to Chester, opened 1795.

(iii)   The Middlewich Branch of the Chester and Ellesmere Canal Company between Barbridge Junction and Middlewich, opened 1833.

(iv)   The Birmingham and Liverpool Junction Canal from Nantwich to Autherley Junction, opened 1835.

The Act for the construction of the Birmingham and Liverpool Canal received royal assent in 1825 and Telford was appointed engineer. The length between Autherley Junction and Nantwich is 39 miles (62km) and the works included a flight of fifteen locks at Audlem, with a total rise or fall of 93ft (28m), a mile (1.6km) long cutting through crumbling rock at Woodseaves and massive embankments at Nantwich, Sheldon and Shelmore. Shelmore embankment was not completed until March 1835, and Telford inspected the works with the contractor, William Corbitt, shortly before his death. Successive earth slips held up the opening of the canal and Telford must have been reminded that construction of the mile (1.6km) long, 60ft (18m) high embankment could have been avoided if Lord Anson had permitted the line of the canal to run through his game preserves in Shelmore Wood (L. T. C. Rolt).

The Birmingham and Liverpool Junction Canal has associations with

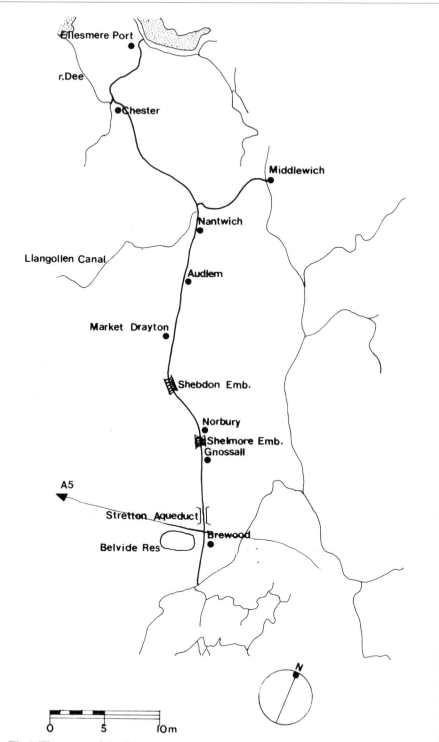

Fig 9 The route of the Birmingham and Liverpool Junction Canal, opened in 1835 several months after Telford's death

Plate 19 Stretton Aqueduct, completed in 1832, carries the Birmingham and Liverpool Junction Canal over the London and Holyhead Road A5(T). Note the alignment of the road (*Derrick Beckett*)

two of Telford's major projects. Just north of Brewood (see Fig 9), the canal crosses the London and Holyhead road via Stretton Aqueduct, which was completed in 1832. The cast-iron structure is shown in Plate 19, which also gives a clear indication of the excellent alignment of the road. The eastern end of Telford's first major canal, the Ellesmere (Llangollen) Canal, links with the Birmingham and Liverpool by a flight of four locks at Hurleston Junction (see Chapter 3).

Fen drainage and navigation has a long history and reference was made in the Introduction to Foss Dyke. The foundation of Lindum Colonia (Lincoln) by Agricola, circa AD 90–6, was followed by the construction of the Car Dyke from the River Nene near Durobrivae (Water Newton), close to Peterborough, to the River Witham at Lincoln. This was extended by the Foss Dyke, length 11 miles (18km), which connected the Witham with the River Trent at Yorksey. It has now been generally established that these waterways were used by the Romans for both drainage and transport and Foss Dyke is Britain's oldest manmade canal still in navigable condition.

Following the departure of the Romans, improvements were made during the reign of Henry I c1120, and in the eighteenth century a number of eminent engineers of the canal era, including James Brindley, John Smeaton, John and Sir John Rennie and Thomas Telford, were actively involved with drainage and navigation improvements of the Fens. Smeaton was consulted on two occasions (1762 and

1782) with regard to improvements to Foss Dyke and subsequently he proposed improvements to the River Nene outfall. John Rennie was extensively involved with the drainage of the Fens between about 1790 and his death in 1821. The essential features of his overall plans for drainage (S. Smiles) were to intercept water flowing into the Fens from higher levels, to improve drainage of the Fen districts themselves and to provide more effective outfalls into the Wash. The outfalls were to be provided with massive sluices which opened outwards, allowing the fresh water to escape into the sea but preventing the sea flowing inland. Telford was associated with John Rennie in improvements to the lower reaches of the River Ouse above King's Lynn. Telford represented the Commissioners for navigation and Rennie the Commissioners for drainage (L. T. C. Rolt), and Eau Brink Cut, which was intended to relieve a bend in the River Ouse above King's Lynn, was completed in 1821. Telford subsequently worked in conjunction with Rennie's son, Sir John Rennie, on the widening of the cut and this was followed by deepening a further 12 miles (19km) of the River Ouse between King's Lynn and Denver near Downham Market.

Telford also worked with Sir John Rennie on improvements to the River Nene outfall from just below Wisbech to Crabs Hole Sluice on the Wash. Between Wisbech and the Wash the South Holland Drain enters the Nene estuary. At this junction accumulation of silt had restricted drainage and navigation and was the reason for an earlier survey by John Rennie in 1814. The Act was not obtained until 1827 and a new cut about 6 miles (10km) long was constructed between 1828 and 1830. This outfall improved flow along the River Nene, and improved drainage released several thousand acres of low-lying fertile land.

Telford's major and last work in the Fens for which he was solely responsible was carried out between 1830 and 1834. This was again in the catchment area of the River Nene, which carries down to the Wash most of the rainfall in Northamptonshire. The area is known as North Level, which is situated to the north-east of Peterborough. It is sandwiched between the rivers Welland and Nene, extending between Crowland (River Welland) and Guyhirn (River Nene), the focal point being Thorney. By constructing a navigable cut known as the New North Level Drain, which ran into the Nene outfall, almost a hundred thousand acres of fertile land were effectively drained. Previously the area was inadequately drained with the assistance of windmills and steam engines.

The effects on the prosperity of the community were immediately apparent — trade at the port of Wisbech doubled, and a humble Fen poet wrote of the moral effects (S. Smiles):

With a change of elements suddenly
There shall a change of men and manners be;
Hearts thick and tough as hides shall feel remorse,
And souls of sedge shall understand discourse;
New hands shall learn to work, forget to steal,
New legs shall go to church, new knees to kneel.

Currently (1986) the Anglian Water Authority is carrying out extensive improvements to the River Nene, emphasising the need for continuing engineering works to maintain adequate flow and drainage in the Fens, a fact which would have been fully appreciated by Telford. Neglect of drainage to the Fens would eventually result in the destruction of an important national asset in both environmental and economic terms.

Thomas Telford died on 2 September 1834, exactly six months before the opening of his last canal, and he was buried in Westminster Abbey. There is a simple diamond-shaped memorial stone in the nave, close to Robert Stephenson's, inscribed 'Thomas Telford (1757–1834)'.

This brief summary of Telford's engineering works over a period of about 60 years hopefully demonstrates his view that '. . . the aim and end of all ought not to be a mere bag of money, but something far higher and far better'. His total estate was £16,000 and his fees were modest: an average of £237 per annum for the Caledonian Canal, £300 for the Ellesmere Canal and £500 for St Katharine Docks. He bequeathed £2,000, his beloved books, drawings and papers to the Institution of Civil Engineers and £850 to his impoverished friend, Robert Southey.

For twenty-one years Telford lived above the Salopian Coffee House at Charing Cross and was a valued customer. On moving into his own property at 24 Abingdon Street, Westminster at the age of 64, Telford greatly disappointed the new landlord of the coffee house, who exclaimed, 'Why, Sir, I have just paid £750 for you' (S. Smiles). Unfortunately, he was suffering from increasing deafness and bouts of sickness, which severely restricted his social life. However, there was some compensation in that he was able to concentrate on his autobiography and the *Atlas* illustrating his works. In contrast to the Stephensons and Brunels, Telford was a bachelor:

It seems singular that with Telford's great natural powers of pleasing, his warm social temperament, and his capability of forming ardent attachments for friends, many of them women, he should never have formed an attachment of the heart. Even in his youthful and poetical days, the subject of love, so frequently the theme of boyish song, is never alluded to; while his school friendships are often recalled to mind and indeed made the special subject of his verse. It seems odd to find him, when at Shrewsbury — a handsome fellow, with a good position, and many beautiful women about him — addressing his friend, the blind schoolmaster at Langholm (Andrew Little) as his 'Stella' . . . (S. SMILES)

However, there were other attachments: to his native Eskdale and childhood friends, his work, books — '. . . knowledge is my most ardent pursuit' — and his fellow engineers. In contrast to France (see Introduction) there was no formal study of engineering science available to young engineers in England until 1826, and in 1817 a group of young engineers was invited by Henry R. Palmer, subsequently one of Telford's assistants on St Katharine Docks, to meet at Kendals Coffee House, London (J. G. Watson). This meeting resulted in the formation of the Institution of Civil Engineers in 1818, with the following aims:

(1) The propounding of discussion of questions of real importance and immediately connected with the pursuits of the profession.
(2) Discussion of the merits of scientific inventions and publications.
(3) The reading and discussion of descriptions of discoveries or researches made by the members.
(4) General communications of any matters or sources of useful information.

In 1820, Telford accepted the invitation to become the first president and subsequently was instrumental in the role that 'each Member shall produce to the Institution at least one unpublished paper each session, a book, map, plan, model or instrument or in failure thereof, shall pay a fine not to become part of the general fund of the Institution, but to be appropriated specifically to the increase of the library'. The current obligation on becoming a corporate member is to present a book to the library or money in lieu.

Telford's love of books was further demonstrated by his bequest to the libraries at Langholm and Westerkirk (see Plate 20).

Telford's views on the requirements for '. . . Youths of respectability and competent education who contemplate Civil Engineering as a profession' are given elsewhere (p8).

His simple upbringing in Eskdale (Plate 21) and early mastery of working with stone and iron influenced the characteristics of subsequent civil engineering works, which in relative terms are comparable with the current £2 billion project for the construction of the Channel Tunnel. A dominant feature of Telford's work is exemplified by James Watt's statement on matters relating to design: '. . . of all things, the supreme excellence is simplicity'.

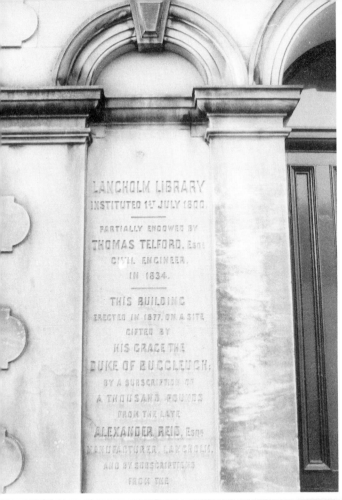

LANGHOLM LIBRARY
INSTITUTED 1ST JULY 1800.

PARTIALLY ENDOWED BY
THOMAS TELFORD, Esqr
CIVIL ENGINEER,
IN 1834.

THIS BUILDING
ERECTED IN 1877, ON A SITE
GIFTED BY
HIS GRACE THE
DUKE OF BUCCLEUCH;
BY A SUBSCRIPTION OF
A THOUSAND POUNDS
FROM THE LATE
ALEXANDER REID, Esqr
MANUFACTURER, LANGHOLM,
AND BY SUBSCRIPTIONS
FROM THE

Plate 20 Langholm Library was partially endowed by Telford (*Derrick Beckett*)

Plate 21 A view across to the River Esk, taken from the rear of the village school opposite the Telford Memorial on the B709 (*Derrick Beckett*)

2

BRIDGES
OVER THE RIVER SEVERN

. . . A greater inundation than has ever been known in England. Much damage and injury has been done by various rivers and the Severn is not behind . . . I have now before me a Plan for one over the Severn at Bewdley in Worcestershire which I have just prepared, and I am likewise drawing one for the town of Bridgnorth, in short I have been at it night and day.

(THOMAS TELFORD)

In the two decades prior to Telford's appointment as architect and surveyor for the county of Shropshire, three important bridges were built over the River Severn, at Shrewsbury (1769–74), Atcham (London and Shrewsbury road, 1768–76) and Coalbrookdale (Iron Bridge, 1778–80). The architect John Gwynn (d1786) was responsible for the seven-span circular stone arch bridge at Shrewsbury. Following numerous delays and contractual problems over a period of about seven years, the bridge was opened in 1774 and cost £14,000. It was rebuilt between 1925 and 1927. Gwynn built a similar seven-span arch bridge at Atcham, which was completed in 1776 at a cost of £7,239. The gradient of the parapets (see Plate 22) should be noted and contrasted with Telford's designs for bridges over the Severn. The gradient and width (18ft) of Atcham bridge was not adequate for the increasing traffic on the London and Shrewsbury road and it is currently used for pedestrian traffic. The road is now carried by a reinforced concrete arch bridge completed in 1929. Some patch repairs have already been carried out and it is unlikely that this bridge will survive for over 200 years as has its stone neighbour.

Of much greater significance was the completion in 1780 of the iron bridge at Coalbrookdale (Plate 23), which forms the centre-piece of Ironbridge Gorge Museum. Although its 100ft (30.6m) span is modest by nineteenth and twentieth century standards, it marked the end of the reign of stone and timber as the dominant materials for bridge construction. It is generally acknowledged to be the first iron bridge in the world. Several people were involved in the design and construction of Iron Bridge, with major contributions from Thomas Pritchard, a Shrewsbury architect and the iron-master Abraham Derby III. The fol-

Plate 22 John Gwynn's bridge over the River Severn at Atcham, completed in 1776 *(Derrick Beckett)*; *(overleaf)* Plate 23 Iron Bridge at Coalbrookdale (1780), the first iron bridge in the world *(Derrick Beckett)*

lowing description of the construction of the bridge is taken from a contemporary account:

The span of the arch is 100 feet 6 inches and the height from the base line to the underside of the arch at the apex is 40 feet. The total weight of iron used in the making of this structure amounted to 378 tons, 10 cwt, the castings being made at the yard of the Coalbrookdale Company . . . The five main ribs were cast in two parts only, approximate length of 70 feet, and of plain rectangular section 9 inches by 7 inches and 9 inches by 6 inches solid . . . The floor 24 feet wide is of open sand cast iron plates, each plate 24 feet by 3 feet 8 inches by 2½ inches flat, not ribbed . . .

Throughout its life, the bridge has suffered from the effects of continuing movement of the abutments, and it was closed to vehicular traffic in 1934. Telford commented that the foundations were either insufficiently massive or inadequately keyed into the rock. From 1950 the abutment movement was continuously monitored and it was eventually found necessary to stabilise the abutments. This was achieved by strutting between the abutments at the level of the river bed and the work was completed in 1974.

The proportions of Iron Bridge copy masonry arches of the same period and the cast-iron circles (see Plate 23) can be compared with the pierced spandrels used by William Edwards in the construction of a stone arch bridge over the River Taff at Pontypridd, which was completed at the fourth attempt in 1756 (see Introduction).

Telford's intense activity in the design and construction of bridges over the River Severn is referred to at the beginning of this chapter: '. . . I have been at it night and day'. Details of Telford's Severn bridges, three of cast iron and three of stone, are listed in Table 3. This excludes

Table 3 Iron Bridge and Telford's stone and cast-iron bridges over the River Severn

Location	Span ft	Span m	Approximate date of construction	Material	Approximate cost £	Fabricator (F) Contractor (C)	Current condition
Iron Bridge, Coalbrookdale	100	30.6	1777–80	Cast iron	6,000	Coalbrookdale Co (F)	Extensive strengthening of foundations, pedestrians only
Montford	50 58 50	15.3 17.7 15.3	1790–2	Stone	5,800	J. Carline & J. Tilley (C)	Widened, carries A5(T)
Buildwas	130	39.7	1795–6	Cast iron	6,170	Coalbrookdale Co (F)	Replaced 1905
Bewdley	52 60 52	15.9 18.3 15.9	1798–9	Stone	8,512	J. Simpson (C)	As built
Mythe, Tewkesbury	170	52.0	1826	Cast iron	14,500	W. Hazledine (F)	Strengthened 1923
Holt Fleet, Ombersley	150	45.8	1827	Cast iron	–	W. Hazledine (F)	Strengthened 1928
Over, Gloucester	150	45.8	1826–30	Stone	43,500	J. Cargill (C)	As built, disused

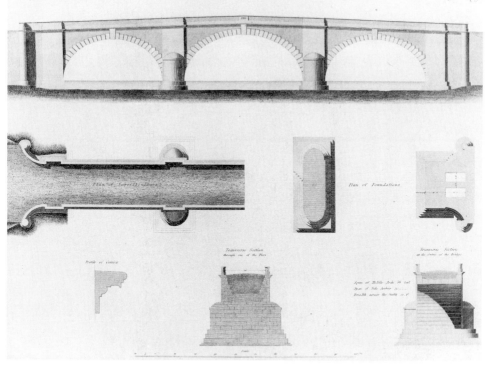

Plate 24 Details of Montford Bridge (1792) (*from* Telford's Atlas, *Richard Packer*)

a timber bridge (J. B. Lawson) which was built across the Severn at Cressage, about 8 miles (13km) south-east of Shrewsbury. It was completed in 1801 at a cost of about £4,000. Telford also refers to his drawing work on a bridge at Bridgnorth, but this did not come to fruition.

Montford Bridge

Telford's first major bridge and his first over the River Severn was constructed between 1790 and 1792 at Montford on the London to Holyhead road, a few miles west of Shrewsbury. Details of the bridge are shown in Plate 24, taken from *Telford's Atlas*.

The three elliptical arches were constructed of red sandstone (Plate 25), which was quarried from Nescliffe Hill about five miles north-west of Montford. The foundations, which were piled, were constructed within cofferdams. Local contractors, John Carline and John Tilley, were responsible for the erection of the arches, much of the labour being undertaken by convicts. Telford's friend, Matthew Davidson from Eskdale, supervised the construction with a local, John Simpson, as mason. Their other work with Telford is referred to elsewhere.

Plate 25 One of the three sandstone arches with the reinforced concrete cantilevered footway above *(Derrick Beckett)*; *(inset)* Plate 26 A close-up of one of the red sandstone voussoirs. The stones were quarried from Nescliffe Hill *(Derrick Beckett)*

In contrast to Telford's later arch bridges, the spandrels are solid (see Plate 24). Plate 26 shows a close-up of the sandstone voussoirs, approximate dimensions 4ft 6in width × 3ft 3in × 2ft in elevation. They were cut with right-angled steps to facilitate building up the spandrel above.

The bridge remains as built but was subsequently widened by the provision of cantilevered footways.

Montford Bridge is an excellent example of the durability of the masonry arch. The current British Standard Code of Practice for bridges, BS 5400, recommends that the useful life of a bridge, with reasonable maintenance, should be 120 years. Telford's design has met this requirement and the bridge carries the heavy vehicles using the A5(T) without weight restriction. His fee for design and supervision was £200.

Buildwas Bridge

By 1790 the medieval bridge at Buildwas, two miles upstream from Iron Bridge, was in an unstable condition resulting from previous landslips. The bridge was largely rebuilt, but collapsed in the floods of 1795.

This presented Telford with the opportunity to design his first iron bridge over the Severn. His proposal was a dramatic departure from the semicircular form of Iron Bridge, as indicated by the details (Plate 27), taken from *Telford's Atlas*.

The form was apparently based on Swiss designs for timber bridges. In 1757, Hans Ulrick Grubenman (1709–83) built a two-span covered timber bridge at Schaffhausen over the Rhine. It was able to sustain loads of up to 25 tons (250kN) and a further single 200ft (61m) span bridge was built by Hans and Johannes Grubenman at Wettingham over the River Limnat near Zurich. The bridges had the appearance of the trussed arch form as with Telford's design for Buildwas. A model was made by the Coalbrookdale Company and the design was subsequently approved. The span was 130ft (40m), 30ft (9m) greater than Iron Bridge, and the weight of iron used less than half, 170 tons.

The light shallow construction had the further advantage that the approach road did not have to be built up on a high embankment. Careful thought was given to the design of the abutments to resist outward thrust. The ironwork was replaced in 1905 but the abutments survive.

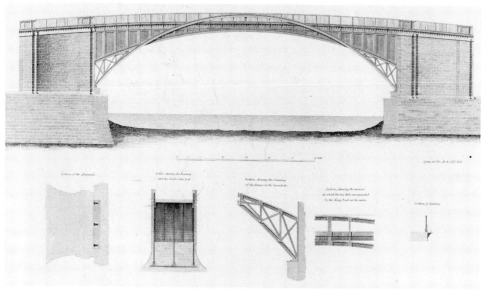

Plate 27 Details of Telford's first iron bridge over the River Severn (*from* Telford's Atlas, *Richard Packer*)

Plate 28 The elegant three-span segmental arch bridge at Bewdley (1798) remains as built *(Derrick Beckett)*; *(right)* Plate 29 A close-up of the voussoirs, showing the recessed spandrel *(Derrick Beckett)*

Bewdley Bridge

As with Buildwas Bridge, the floods of 1795 led to Telford being appointed to design a new bridge at Bewdley in Worcestershire. Samuel Smiles recalls that Telford wrote to a friend in December 1798:

We have had a remarkably dry summer and autumn; after that an early fall of snow and some frost, followed by rain. The drought of the summer was unfavourable to our canal building; but it has enabled us to raise Bewdley Bridge as if by enchantment. We have thus built a magnificent bridge over the Severn in one season, which is no contemptible work for John Simpson and your humble servant, amidst so many other great undertakings. John Simpson is a treasure — a man of great talents and integrity. I met him here by chance, employed and recommended him, and he has now under his charge all the works of any magnitude in this rich and great district.

Telford was justifiably proud of his bridge at Bewdley (Plate 28) and its elegance rivals that of Dunkeld Bridge completed ten years later (see Chapter 8). The Georgian waterfront at Bewdley is a perfect setting for the bridge and the author well remembers visiting it on a warm late summer's day with the Severn unusually tranquil.

The arch spans are similar to Montford, but in contrast a segmental form was adopted. The voussoirs are emphasised (Plate 29) by recessing the spandrels and its appearance is enhanced by the slight upward cur-

vature of the parapet. The stone was quarried at Arley about four miles upstream and as with Montford Bridge the pier foundations were constructed within cofferdams. However, they were not piled as rock was found a few feet below the river. The bridge remains as built and represents remarkable value at a cost of less than £9,000.

Mythe and Holt Fleet Bridges

A distance of 20 miles (32km) separates two cast-iron bridges with similar framing to earlier bridge structures built for the Highlands road system described in Chapter 8. Mythe Bridge near Tewkesbury has the largest span of Telford's cast-iron bridges, 170ft (52m), but, as we have seen, Telford was involved as early as 1800 in a proposal for a span of over three times this for a new London bridge. An earlier design for a three-span arch bridge was prepared in 1820 by a local architect, following an Act for the construction of a bridge at Tewkesbury. The design was rejected. Telford was appointed by the trustees to prepare an alternative design and construction work started in 1823. The iron founder was William Hazledine and the segments of Shropshire iron were cast at his Shrewsbury factory. Hazledine's previous experience with Telford in Scotland (see Chapter 8) must have been invaluable in the design and construction of the ironwork, but the bridge took a surprisingly long time to build. It was not completed until the spring of 1826. The six arch ribs, cast in segments about 3ft 3in deep (1.0m), with a span of 170ft (52m) and rise of 17ft (5.2m), and connected to the deck by spandrels with light diagonal framing, give the bridge a delicate and elegant

appearance as indicated in Plate 30. An interesting feature of the embankments is that they are pierced by narrow Gothic flood arches. On the eastern approaches there is a picturesque toll-house (Plate 31) and its style contrasts with the more severe and functional designs adopted on the London and Holyhead road and elsewhere (see Chapter 3). The cost of the ironwork was about 30 per cent of the total construction cost of £14,500. This figure reflects the relatively high cost of the approach works and foundations. Mythe Bridge was strengthened in 1923.

Holt Fleet Bridge, Worcestershire, was completed in 1827 and strengthened in 1928 (Plate 32). Its span of 150ft (46m) is identical to Bonar (1812), Craigellachie (1815) and Galton (1829), thus utilising over a period of about twenty years a standardised design, a technique frequently adopted in recent years for reinforced and prestressed concrete motorway bridges.

Over Bridge, Gloucester

At Gloucester, Telford was not able to utilise his 'standard' 150ft (46m) span in cast iron. Local dignitaries were against the use of cast iron and Telford designed a single-span stone arch maintaining the 150ft (46m) span. Telford's design was based on the arch form developed by Perronet. As we have seen (Introduction), Perronet was the first director of the Ecole des Ponts et Chaussées and was responsible for the construction of numerous bridges, including the Pont Neuilly crossing the Seine below Paris. Neuilly Bridge consisted of five 130ft (40m) span arches, each with a 30ft (9m) rise. The main body of the arches was approximately elliptical in form but the outer faces were segmental in form and the difference in curvature, which increased towards the abutments, was taken up by a bevelled inward slope. This effect can be clearly seen in the Over Bridge (see Plate 33), the bevelled appearance of the voussoirs tapering towards the crown of the arch. These were known as '*cornes de vache*' or cow's horns (T. Ruddock). Telford was not the first British engineer to copy Perronet's design. It was used by George Dodds in 1809 in a proposal for constructing Waterloo Bridge to link the Strand near Somerset House with the south bank of the Thames at Lambeth. This proposal was examined by John Rennie and William Jessop, and Samuel Smiles refers to their report on the design:

Plate 30 Mythe Bridge, Telford's largest cast-iron span, 170ft (52m). The embankments are pierced by narrow flood arches *(Derrick Beckett)*; *(inset)* Plate 31 The toll-house at Mythe Bridge *(Derrick Beckett)*

Plate 32 Holt Fleet Bridge undergoing maintenance, August 1984 *(Derrick Beckett)*

We should not have thought it necessary to quote the production of a foreign country for the sake of showing the practicability of constructing arches of 130 feet span, had we not been led to it by the exact similarity of the designs, and by the principle which is therein adopted of the compound curve; because our own country affords examples of greater boldness in the construction of arches than that at Neuilly. There is a bridge over the river Taff, in the county of Glamorgan, of upwards of 135 feet span, with a rise not exceeding 32 feet, and what is more remarkable is, that the depth of the arch stones is only 30 inches; so that in fact that bridge far exceeds in boldness of design that at Neuilly.

The bridge over the River Taff at Pontypridd was designed by William Edwards, a preacher, farmer and mason (see Introduction) and Rennie and Jessop did not state in their report that the bridge at Pontypridd, which was completed in 1756, could only be made stable at the fourth attempt to construct it: the three previous constructions collapsed.

Rennie and Jessop went on to criticise Neuilly Bridge further:

. . . for when the centres of the bridge at Neuilly were struck, the top of the arches sank to a degree far beyond anything that has come to our knowledge, whilst the haunches retired or rose up, so that the bridge as it now stands is very different in form from what was originally designed. No such change took place in the bridge over the Taff; the sinking after the centres were struck did not amount to one-half of that at Neuilly, although the one was designed and built under the direction of the first engineer of France without regard to expense, whilst the other was designed and built by a country mason with parsimonious economy.

William Edwards' bridge still stands through luck or 'God's blessing' and English–French rivalry in other than political matters is immediately apparent in Jessop and Rennie's report.

Needless to say, George Dodds' design was abandoned and Waterloo Bridge was eventually opened in June 1817 to the design of John Rennie. Rennie declined a knighthood: 'I had a hard business to escape a knighthood at the opening' and according to Smiles '. . . we believe that not a crack is visible in the entire work'.

To return to the Over Bridge which was erected between 1826 and 1830, Telford chose to ignore Rennie's comments on Neuilly Bridge and commented on the form of his bridge as follows:

This complex form converts each side of the vault of the arch into the shape of the entrance of a pipe, to suit the contracted passage of a fluid, thus lessening the flat surface opposed to the current of the river whenever the tide or upland flood rises above the springing of the middle of the ellipse, that being four feet above low water; whereas the flood of 1770 rose twenty feet above low water of an ordinary spring-tide, which, when there is no upland flood, rises only eight or nine feet.

Plate 33 The *'cornes de vache'* at Over Bridge (*Derrick Beckett*)

Over Bridge is the second largest remaining masonry arch bridge in Britain, the largest being Grosvenor Bridge at Chester, completed in 1833 with a span of 200ft (61m). The general body of the arch is an ellipse of 35ft (10.7m) rise, whereas on the face the rise is only 13ft (4m), giving the funnel effect referred to previously.

In his *Life* Telford refers to Neuilly Bridge: 'For this bridge of one stone arch I introduced a form which, although a novelty in England, had, in 1768 been employed by an eminent French architect (Mr. Perronet) . . . and this appeared to be peculiarly applicable to the Severn where the upland floods are considerable'.

The masonry is sandstone and was quarried at Arley (see the section on Bewdley Bridge) and transported by river to the site. In a similar manner to Mythe Bridge, excavation on the river banks was taken down to what Telford assumed to be a thick gravel bed at a depth of 33ft (10m) on the eastern bank and 27ft (8m) on the western bank (J. Heyman). In a paper presented to the Institution of Civil Engineers in November 1972, Heyman states that Telford was probably misled by the soil data made available to him. Recent soil surveys indicate that on the eastern (Gloucester) bank, a thin layer of sand and pebbles at a depth of about 32–3ft (10m) overlies a layer of soft clay. The abutments were not piled and their foundations consisted of a layer of rubble placed on what was thought to be a gravel bed, above which was placed a timber platform of

Plate 34 Until recently Over Bridge carried main road traffic. It now stands in splendid isolation (*Derrick Beckett*)

Memel pine logs placed at 3ft (0.9m) centres. The spaces between the logs were filled with rubble, upon which were placed beech planks, 4in (100mm) thick. This provided a platform 40ft (12m) × 37ft (11m), from which massive abutments were built up to contain the arch thrust. Although the arches are partially hollow, their self-weight is much greater than for cast-iron bridges of a similar span. For example, the cast-iron arches for Holt Fleet Bridge weigh only 180 tons (1800kN) and the total cost was £8,512 compared with £43,500 for Over Bridge. This high cost is indicative of an uneconomic design and extensive construction problems.

On removal of the arch centring, the crown sank 10in (250mm) but it is worth noting that the crown of Neuilly Bridge sank 23½in (600mm) on decentring.

Between 1830 and 1832 Telford was required to carry out repairs to cracks, and the bridge has a history of continuing crack propagation. Records of cracks have been kept by Gloucestershire County Council since 1908. In his paper, Heyman provides a summary of calculations to assess the stability of the bridge and states that the bridge is acting as a three-hinged arch (see Appendix). Until recently, Over Bridge carried main road traffic, the A40(T), but now stands in splendid isolation (Plate 34) as a result of the construction of a new road network round Gloucester.

Telford was involved in the design and construction of bridges over the River Severn for a period of 40 years (1790–1830) and the fact that five of them are still standing, one of which carries trunk road traffic (Montford), is a remarkable tribute to his ability to design bridges for both strength and durability. With the materials available to him, he wisely chose the arch form in masonry and cast iron.

3
ELLESMERE CANAL AND
THE PONT CYSYLLTE AQUEDUCT

. . . And thus has been added a striking feature to the beautiful vale of Llangollen, where formerly was the fastness of Owen Glendower, but which, now cleared of its entangled woods, contains a useful line of intercourse between England and Ireland, and the water drawn from the once sacred Devon furnishes the means of distributing prosperity over the adjacent land of the Saxons.

(THOMAS TELFORD)

The 'line of intercourse' referred to by Telford was the Ellesmere Canal, opened in 1805 following the completion of the Pont Cysyllte Aqueduct over the River Dee near Llangollen.

The Ellesmere Canal (now called the Llangollen Canal) originated from plans to link the rivers Severn and Mersey by means of a canal with access to iron and coal fields in the vicinity of Shrewsbury, Ellesmere and Ruabon. From about 1790 two rival schemes were promoted, known as the eastern and western routes. The eastern route was intended to link the rivers Mersey and Severn by a line running to the east of the River Dee with a western branch to serve the iron and coal fields. This avoided the difficult terrain of the western route which followed a line to the west of the River Dee, running from Chester, skirting Wrexham and then on to Ruabon, Chirk and Shrewsbury.

In 1791, William Jessop was appointed to report on the two rival schemes and preferred the western route. In the following year he proposed a route (C. Hadfield and A. W. Skempton) which crossed the Wirral from the Mersey to the Dee, ran to the east of Wrexham and then on to Ruabon. It crossed the Dee at Pont Cysyllte, the Ceirog near Chirk and continued via Frankton to join the Severn at Shrewsbury. Jessop's route was considered by the promoters and it was accepted following modifications to avoid a 13,800ft (4,220m) long tunnel near Ruabon. The Act for the construction of the canal was passed on 30 April 1793 and by 1796 the section across the Wirral between the Mersey and the Dee (Ellesmere Port and Chester) was open and carried heavy traffic — goods and passengers. This section could accommodate boats of 14ft (4.3m) beam. In the same year a branch from Frankton (see Fig 10) to

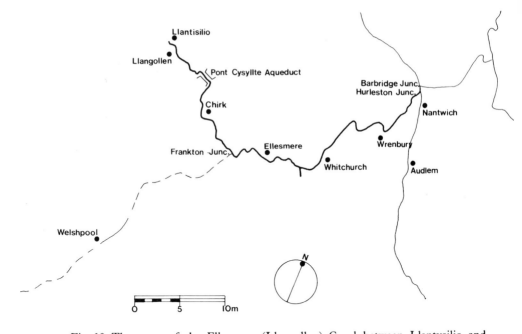

Fig 10 The route of the Ellesmere (Llangollen) Canal between Llantysilio and Hurleston Junction

Llangmynech was completed: this now forms part of the disused Montgomeryshire Canal which is currently being partially restored.

The sections between Chester and Ruabon and Frankton were not built and thus the connection between the Severn and Mersey was not achieved. Fig 10 shows the route of the Ellesmere Canal as used today and by 1805 this route was open between Llangollen and Hurleston, on the Chester Canal (now Shropshire Union). It is arguably the most popular cruising canal in the country and it crosses the rivers Ceirog and Dee via two spectacular aqueducts which were designed by William Jessop and Thomas Telford.

As we have seen, Jessop was appointed engineer to the canal company in 1791, but it was not until September 1793 that Telford was appointed 'General Agent, Surveyor, Engineer, Architect and Overlooker of the Works to make Reports to superintend the cutting forming and making the Canal and taking up and seeing the due observance of the levels thereof to make the Drawings and to submit such Drawings to the Consideration and Correction of Mr. William Jessop . . . His engagement to extend to all Architecture and Engineering Business to the Drawings forming and directing the making of Bridges, Aqueducts Tunnels Locks Buildings Reservoirs Wharfs and other works' (C. Hadfield and A. W. Skempton).

This is a most revealing job description and indicates Telford's position in relation to Jessop, who held overall responsibility for the works. Telford's appointment was part-time at a salary of £300 per annum, as in 1793 he still retained his post as surveyor of public works for Shropshire (see Chapter 1).

The aqueducts at Chirk and Pont Cysyllte are the dominant civil engineering works on the 44 mile (70km) route between Hurleston Junction and Llangollen. In a report to the canal committee written in July 1795, Jessop proposed iron aqueducts for crossing the Dee and the Chirk Valley. Four months prior to this, Telford wrote to Andrew Little (see Chapter 1) informing him of his recommendation for an iron aqueduct at Longdon on Tern. Further, Telford's cast-iron bridge at Buildwas (see Chapter 2) was in the course of construction. Thus there was abundant confidence in the structural potential of cast iron, but surprisingly, in February 1796, Telford consulted Jessop and they agreed to use masonry arches instead of an iron trough for the aqueduct at Chirk. The aqueduct is 696ft (213m) long, 70ft (21m) high and has ten arches of 40ft (12m) span. The view shown in Plate 35, looking down to the aqueduct, is taken from the B4500 where it crosses the entrance to the 1,380ft (422m) long Chirk Tunnel (see Gazetteer, p162).

Plate 35 A view looking down onto Chirk Aqueduct from the B4500 where it crosses the entrance to Chirk Tunnel (*Derrick Beckett*)

Construction of the arches was completed by November 1799 and the spandrels were not solid, but were constructed with five longitudinal walls. Telford's autobiography provides an interesting description of the construction:

Telford himself thus modestly describes the merit of this original contrivance: 'Previously to this time such canal aqueducts had been uniformly made to retain the water necessary for navigation by means of puddled earth retained by masonry; and in order to obtain sufficient breadth for this superstructure, the masonry of the piers, abutments, and arches was of massive strength; and after all this expense, and every imaginable precaution, the frosts, by swelling the moist puddle, frequently created fissures, which burst the masonry; and suffered the water to escape — nay, sometimes actually threw down the aqueducts; instances of this kind having occurred even in the works of the justly celebrated Brindley. It was evident that the increased pressure of the puddled earth was the chief cause of such failures: I therefore had recourse to the following scheme in order to avoid using it. The spandrels of the stone arches were constructed with longitudinal walls, instead of being filled in with earth (as at Kirkcudbright Bridge), and across these the canal bottom was formed by cast iron plates at each side, infixed in square stone masonry. These bottom plates had flanches on their edges, and were secured by nuts and screws at every juncture. The sides of the canal were made water-proof by ashlar masonry, backed with hard burnt bricks laid in Parker's cement, on the outside of which was rubble stone work, like the rest of the aqueduct. The towing path had a thin bed of clay under the gravel, and its outer edge was protected by an iron railing. The width of the water-way is 11 feet; of the masonry on each side, 5 feet 6 inches; and the depth of the water in the canal, 5 feet. By this mode of construction the quantity of masonry is much diminished, and the iron bottom plate forms a continuous tie, preventing the side-walls from separation by lateral pressure of the contained water . . .'

It appears that the decision to use cast-iron plates to form the canal bottom was not made until the latter stages of construction. The plates were cast at William Hazledine's Plas Kynaston ironworks and delivered during the summer of 1800. The aqueduct was opened to traffic during 1801 and the works commenced on 17 June 1796 (S. Smiles). Subsequently (date unknown), the channel was lined completely with an iron trough, the original bottom plate being broken out. It is possible to gain access to the space between the spandrel walls by means of a 2ft (0.6m) square hole at just above the springing level of each arch. Over the years water has seeped into the structure, washing away the lime mortar, resulting in some movement and cracking of the stonework. As with the Pont Cysyllte Aqueduct, which is of similar age, long-term deterioration has to be carefully monitored.

It was indicated previously that Jessop's report of July 1795 recommended an iron aqueduct for crossing the River Dee. The foundation stone to the Pont Cysyllte Aqueduct was laid on 25 July 1795 and it was eventually opened over ten years later on 21 November 1805. The aqueduct can be described objectively as having an overall span of 1,007ft (308m) with nineteen cast-iron arches with clear spans of 45ft (14m). Plate 36 shows thirteen of the nineteen arches and the approach embankment 1,500ft (459m) in length and reaching 97ft (30m) in height can be seen to the right of the photograph. The view shown in

Plate 36 Thirteen of the nineteen arches of Pont Cysyllte Aqueduct can be seen from this view with the south abutment on the right. The River Dee is out of sight on the far left (*Derrick Beckett*)

Plate 37 is taken from the abutment at the tip of the south embankment looking north towards the River Dee. The construction details are clearly shown, the 11ft 10in (3.6m) wide trough being supported on four cast-iron arch ribs. The iron trough was formed from flanged cast-iron plates bolted together and the inclination of the flanged joints on the vertical plates forming the sides of the trough is similar to that of a flat masonry arch used to form door and window openings in buildings. The joints were made watertight with Welsh flannel and lead. The most spectacular impression of the scale of the aqueduct can be obtained by standing at the top of the south abutment and looking along the canal towards the River Dee (see Plate 38). Leakage from the aqueduct has not been a problem and the British Waterways Board's primary concern is the possibility of a 30 ton (300kN) canal boat hitting the trough wall and causing a fracture. However, an interesting comparison can be made with the aqueduct at Longdon on Tern (see Plate 8, p40). At Longdon the towpath was placed outside the trough whereas the Pont Cysyllte has a towpath which cantilevers out into the trough, as can be seen in Fig 5. As a boat moves along the trough, the water displaced at the bow moves under the towpath towards the stern and there is a consequent reduction in level below that in the section through which the boat passes. The effect of this is to induce a lateral force on the boat which causes it to move towards the edge of the towpath, thus reducing the possibility of the unprotected wall of the trough being nudged. It is a matter of conjecture as to whether this was reasoned by Telford or Jessop, or just chance. William Hazledine's foundry at Plas Kynaston close to Pont Cysyllte enabled him to obtain the contract for the ironwork in March 1802. Hazledine was responsible for the casting, transport and erection of the ironwork. In 1978 settlement of the south abutment caused distortion of the cast-iron ribs on the first span and they were replaced. One of the ribs (see Plate 39) is exhibited at the Waterways Museum (see Gazetteer, p177).

Plate 37 The four ribs which support the cast-iron trough are clearly seen in this view of Pont Cysyllte, taken from the south abutment, towpath side. Note the handrail above the trough (*Derrick Beckett*)

Plate 38 Looking along the trough from the south abutment. The pedestrian is protected by a substantial handrail, but for those crossing by boat there are just a few inches from the water level to the top of the trough and a 130ft (40m) drop to the River Dee (*Derrick Beckett*)

Plate 39 One of the cast-iron ribs of Pont Cysyllte exhibited at the Waterways Museum, Stoke Bruerne. It was replaced following settlement of the south abutment (*Derrick Beckett*)

Plate 40 A typical timber lift bridge (Fron lift bridge no 28). It is close to the embankment which takes the canal up to the south abutment of the Pont Cysyllte Aqueduct (*Derrick Beckett*); (*above*) Plate 41 Bridge 70 (should be 1) is typical of thousands of hump-backed masonry arches built to carry roads over canals (*Derrick Beckett*)

Erection of the slender masonry piers supporting the cast-iron arches presented a formidable task as they reached a height of 126ft (38m) at the River Dee. Matthew Davidson supervised the work and the construction of the piers was a matter of concern for Jessop, who wrote to Telford in July 1795 (C. Hadfield and A. W. Skempton): 'In looking forward to the time when we shall be laying the Iron Trough on the Piers I forsee some difficulties that appear to be formidable — In the first place I see men giddy and terrified in laying stones with such an immense depth underneath them'.

The piers were solid to a height of 70ft (21m) and then continued in cellular form with 2ft (0.6m) thick outer walls and cross walls between them. Pont Cysyllte Aqueduct was built at a cost of about £47,000 — about £3.95 per square foot, an enviable figure to those involved in bridge construction today.

The Chirk and Pont Cysyllte aqueducts overshadow a number of interesting features of the Ellesmere Canal. Construction of a navigable feeder between Pont Cysyllte and Llantysilio (see Gazetteer, p160) was sanctioned in 1804. It ran for six miles along the north side of the Vale of Llangollen where it was supplied with water from the River Dee at Horseshoe Falls. This work was completed in 1808. The flow of water towards Hurleston is about eight million gallons a day and now supplies a reservoir adjacent to Hurleston Junction.

Bridge 28, numbered from Frankton Junction, is typical of a number of counterbalanced timber lift bridges to be found on the canal (see Plate 40). This bridge is close to the winding hole beyond which the canal is carried on a tree-lined embankment up to the south abutment of the Pont Cysyllte Aqueduct. A typically tranquil stretch of the Ellesmere Canal is shown in Plate 41. The hump-backed masonry arch bridge with the plaque numbered 70 is typical of thousands of bridges built to carry roads over the canals. The bridges were numbered 1 to 69 from Hurleston Junction up to Frankton Junction. The numbering begins again beyond the junction and thus bridge 70 should be bridge 1. It will be recalled that one of the original lines proposed for the Ellesmere Canal from Chester to Shrewsbury ran from Frankton to Shrewsbury. The Shrewsbury section branched off four locks down from Frankton Junction (see Plate 80, p162). The section from Frankton to Shrewsbury continued for a few miles and work was abandoned. Another branch was completed as far as Llanmynech, and then joined the Montgomeryshire Canal. The canal from Frankton Junction to Llanmynech has now been renamed the Montgomeryshire Canal and partial restoration is in hand.

4

LONDON AND HOLYHEAD ROAD

This road established through a rugged and mountainous district, partly along the slope of rocky precipices, and across inlets of the sea, where mail and other coaches are now enabled to travel at the rate of nine or ten miles an hour, was indeed an arduous undertaking, which occupied fifteen years of incessant exertion.

(THOMAS TELFORD)

It will be recalled from the Introduction, that compared with coach speeds in the middle of the eighteenth century, a rate of nine or ten miles an hour represented a significant improvement and exemplifies Telford's ability in the planning and construction of major roads. Sir Henry Parnell, MP for Queens County, in his *Treatise on Roads* (1833) referred to the Holyhead Road improvement scheme as 'a model of the most perfect road making that has ever been attempted in any Country'.

The Act of Union between the Parliaments of England and Ireland in 1800 focused attention on the need to improve communications between the two countries. The time to cross the frequently storm-tossed Irish Sea could be considerably reduced by crossing from Dublin to Holyhead rather than Liverpool. However, the 24 mile (38km) road across Anglesey to the Menai Strait was no more than a circuitous rocky track (S. Smiles) and this was followed by an open ferry grappling with rapid tides and strong winds. The condition of the road between Bangor and Shrewsbury, and those in Wales generally, was no better than that across Anglesey and Smiles states that '. . . in 1803, when the late Lord Sudeley took home his bride from the neighbourhood of Welshpool to his residence only thirteen miles distant, the carriage in which the newly married pair rode stuck in a quagmire, and the occupants having extracted themselves from their perilous situation, performed the rest of their journey on foot'.

The following optimistic advertisement appeared in the *Shrewsbury Chronicle*, 3 April 1801:

Thirty years later, following the completion of the bulk of Telford's improvements to the Holyhead Road, a coach service was advertised on 1 July 1831:

The difference in travelling times is indicative of the vast improvement in travelling conditions resulting from massive engineering works directed by Thomas Telford between 1815 and 1830. The state of the road in 1815 was described in evidence put before a House of Commons Committee (S. Smiles):

'Many parts of the road are extremely dangerous for a coach to travel upon. At several places between Bangor and Capel-Curig there are a number of dangerous precipices without fences, exclusive of various hills that want taking down. At Ogwen Pool there is a very dangerous place where the water runs over the road, extremely difficult to pass at flooded times. Then there is Dinas Hill, that needs a side fence against a deep precipice. The width of the road is not above twelve feet in the steepest part of the hill, and two carriages cannot pass without the greatest danger. Between this hill and Rhyddlanfair there are a number of dangerous precipices, steep hills, and difficult narrow turnings. From Corwen to Llangollen the road is very narrow, long, and steep; has no side fence, except about a foot and a half of mould or dirt, which is thrown up to prevent carriages falling down three or four hundred feet into the river Dee. Stage-coaches have been frequently overturned and broken down from the badness of the road, and the mails have been overturned; but I wonder that more and worse accidents have not happened, the roads are so bad.' — Evidence of Mr. William Akers, of the Post-Office, before Committee of the House of Commons, 1st June, 1815.

Following years of lobbying, a parliamentary committee was set up in 1810 to investigate the need for improvements to the Holyhead road and Telford was called upon to prepare a report, but no action was taken on his recommendations which, needless to say, proposed extensive realignment and widening. This had to wait until the Holyhead Road Commission was appointed in 1815.

As we have seen, the main roads in England and Wales were administered by a largely ineffective turnpike system and the tolls raised were completely inadequate to meet the improvements recommended by Telford. However, the Holyhead Road Commission had considerable sums of government money at its disposal and with Telford as engineer this money was used to great effect. The work was divided into two sections: London to Shrewsbury and Shrewsbury to Holyhead. The Shrewsbury to Holyhead section required a much greater expenditure and expertise to improve travelling conditions such that coach speeds of 10mph could be achieved. The roadworks were overshadowed by the construction of the Menai Suspension Bridge (1818–26), which is described in Chapter 4. This is in a way regrettable, as, arguably, the civil engineering works directed by Telford between Shrewsbury and Holyhead, involving almost complete reconstruction of the existing road, are the finest example of his immense and catholic ability. The road has survived virtually unchanged, whereas the Menai Bridge suffered structural damage a week after it was opened.

Work on the Welsh section commenced in October 1815 and one of the first sections to be completed was at Betwys-y-Coed, which involved the construction of Waterloo Bridge over the River Conwy (see Plate

Plates 42, 43 and 44 Features of Waterloo Bridge — decorations of roses, leeks, thistles and shamrocks, and the acknowledgement of William Hazledine and William Stuttle (*Richard Jewell*)

42). Waterloo Bridge is one of a number of notable cast-iron arch bridges built by Telford (see Chapter 2), but differs from the others in that it has decorated spandrels with roses, thistles, leeks and shamrocks cast in (Plate 43). An inscription states that 'this arch was constructed the same year the battle of Waterloo was fought'. In fact, it was not completed until 1816. Of much greater significance is the acknowledgement of the iron founder, William Hazledine and the foreman, William Stuttle (Plate 44). This is a rare tribute, as generally, acknowledgement plaques on bridges relate to local dignitaries who have no responsibility whatsoever for design or construction.

One of the most hazardous sections of the road referred to by Telford as 'the most dreadful horsepath in Wales' (B. Trinder) was the route beyond the west end of Lake Ogwen through the Nant Ffrancon pass. Plate 45 shows the bridge beyond the west end of Lake Ogwen (see Gazetteer, p163). The road was then cut through the side of the mountain (Plate 46) en route to Bangor. A new road, completed in 1822, was constructed across Anglesey. At Stanley Sands near Holyhead, Telford constructed a 3,900ft (1,192m) long embankment 34ft (10.4m) wide at

Plate 45 The bridge beyond the west end of Lake Ogwen (*Derrick Beckett*)

Plate 46 The road running along the side of the mountain, en route to Bangor (*Derrick Beckett*)

the top and 114ft (35m) wide at the bottom. This major engineering work saved a distance of 1½ miles (2.4km) in the overall length of the Anglesey road.

Work on the English section commenced in 1819, but one important river crossing, over the River Severn at Montford, a few miles west of Shrewsbury, was completed in 1792 (see Chapter 2). Montford Bridge still carries the London to Holyhead (A5(T)) traffic and demonstrates the long-term durability of the masonry arch. The English section did not require engineering works comparable with the Welsh section, but the general condition of the road surface was poor and extensive realignment and reduction of gradients was necessary to achieve a standard comparable with the rebuilt Welsh section.

Prior to the improvements on the Holyhead road, Telford accumulated extensive experience of road and bridge construction in Scotland, where he was responsible for the completion of a 1,000 mile (1,600km) network. This experience influenced the technical features of the Holyhead road, the most important of which was provision of well-drained and durable carriageway. The construction details of the carriageway were stated by Telford as follows:

Upon the level bed prepared for the road materials the bottom course, or layer of stone, is to be set by hand in the form of a close, firm pavement. They are to be set on the broadest edges, lengthwise across the road, and the breadth of the upper beds is not to exceed 4 inches in any case. All the irregularities of the upper part of the said pavement are to be broken off by a hammer, and all the interstices to be filled with stone chips, firmly wedged together by hand with a light hammer. The middle 18 feet of pavement is to be coated with hard stone as nearly cubical as possible, broken to go through a 2½-inch ring, to a depth of 6 inches, 4 of these 6 inches to be first put on and worked by traffic, after which the remaining 2 inches can be put on. The work of setting the paving-stones must be executed with the greatest care and strictly according to the foregoing directions, or otherwise the stone will become loose and in time may work up to the surface of the road. When the work is properly executed, no stone can move; the whole of the material to be covered with 1½ inches of good gravel, free from clay or earth.

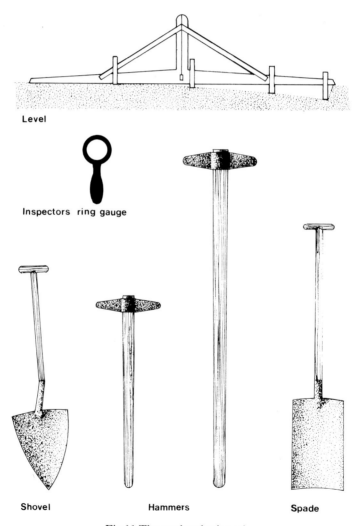

Level

Inspectors ring gauge

Shovel   Hammers   Spade

Fig 11 The road maker's tools

The ring gauge referred to above is illustrated in Fig 11, along with other road makers' tools. All Telford's engineering works were constructed by hand, with the exception of the Caledonian Canal (Chapter 7) and St Katharine Docks (Chapter 6), where steam engines were employed to pump water from excavations.

The level was used to maintain a road surface camber of 1 in 60 to ensure water flowed off the surface into adjacent ditches. The curved blade of the spade facilitated the removal of stiff clay and the curved handle of the shovel allowed the workmen to bring the blade flat to the ground without stooping.

Other important technical improvements were the easing of gradients, which were as steep as 1 in 6½, down to 1 in 20 and widening the carriageway to between 30ft (9.2m) and 40ft (12.2m).

The Holyhead road was constructed with an *élan* comparable with the works of the most charismatic of Victorian engineers, Isambard Kingdom Brunel. Characteristic features are the milestones (see Plate 84, p167). These were quarried from Red Wharf Bay (B. Trinder) on the east coast of Anglesey. They cost £5 each to install and weighed over a ton.

Telford maintained that he could not find a milestone he could copy, but the Romans used milestones (miliaria) every thousand paces along their highways, some of which remain in England.

An architectural feature of the Holyhead road is the toll-house, fifteen of which were constructed between Shrewsbury and Holyhead. On the mainland they were of single-storey construction (Plate 47), and in Anglesey, they were built with a tower bedroom (see Gazetteer, p164). The Shelton toll-house is preserved at the Iron Gorge Museum and the specification for its construction is given below:

Specification for Building a Toll-House at Shelton, in the Parish of St. Chad, in the County of Salop.

The whole of the walls, except the plinth, steps, and window sills, are to be of good sound brick-work, to be laid solid in good mortar, composed of lime and sand; and the outer joints to be neatly struck with the trowel. The plinth, steps, and window sills to be of neatly tooled freestone.

The rooms numbered 1 and 2 on the plan are to be floored with paving tile, well bedded in mortar. Those numbered 3 and 4 are to have joints of batten fir, sixteen inches from centre to centre, seven inches deep, and two inches and a half thick, and to be covered with wrought-inch board of fir or poplar. All the ceilings to have joists not less than three inches by two inches, and the roof to have rafters of the same dimensions, with purloins four inches square under the whole of them. The ceiling, joists, and rafters to be sixteen inches from centre to centre. Hips and ridges to be one inch and a half by eight inches, and

raised to receive the lead. The wall plates to be four inches and a half by two inches and a half.

The roof to be covered with good slate, nailed on two-inch sawn lath, and to be rough-rendered inside. All the hips and ridges to be covered with lead, fifteen inches wide, and not less than five pounds to the foot, and valleys not less than six pounds to the foot.

All ceilings to be plastered on heart lath, two coats, floated and set.

Walls to have two coats, rendered and set. The under side of the portico and projection of the roof to be also ceiled and plastered, and faced with a three inch and a half fascia board.

All ceilings and plastered walls to be whitewashed, to have six-inch skirting round all the rooms, of fir, one inch thick.

Outer door frames to be of oak, four inches square. The front door to be two inches thick, six-panelled, square, and rusticated. The back door to be of one inch and a half deal, ledged, ploughed, tongued, and beaded.

Inner door frames to be of fir, not less than four inches by three inches. Inner doors of one and a half inch fir, six-panelled. Window frames to have oak sills, and the rest of the framing to be of fir, glazed with best second diamond fashion in lead, with quartered oak casements, and iron saddle bars.

There is to be a five eighth of an inch beaded angle staff at every external angle of the plastering.

All timber work, except where otherwise expressed, to be of Baltic fir.

The porch to be supported with oak or larch poles. All the timber work usually painted to be painted three times in oil. The inner doors and skirtings to be finished chocolate colour; the rest of the interior to be white; all the outside to be painted dark green.

Grates must be fixed in the fireplaces, each of which must have stone hearths, jambs, and mantels.

All doors and windows to have proper locks, hangings, and fastenings; and the whole house to be finished in a complete and workmanlike manner.

A privy must be built near the house, with proper seats, roof, door, &c. complete, to be placed in such situations as may be pointed out by the commissioners' engineer or his assistant.

A number of gates installed at the toll-houses were of rising sun design (Plate 48).

To appreciate the excellence of the Holyhead road, it is necessary to travel along it (see Gazetteer, p163); the 260 mile (416km) journey will be well rewarded if thought is given to fifteen years of 'incessant exertion'.

Plate 47 A single-storey toll-house on the A5(T) (*Derrick Beckett*)

Plate 48 A toll-gate of 'rising sun' design at the approach to the Menai Suspension Bridge (*Derrick Beckett*)

5

MENAI AND CONWY BRIDGES

This immense work, which in all its parts is regulated by the principle of utility, is totally deficient in all the charms of beauty. It cuts the landscape like a black uniform line, uneven on one side, and perfectly horizontal on the other; and when viewed closely, the columns by which the bridge is supported, are wholly destitute of every description of architectural or sculptural ornament. These perpetually recurring iron rods, which follow one another in monotonous rows, only serve to suggest the feeling of despair to which a painter must be reduced in any attempt to delineate the structure, and to give anything like an accurate drawing of this tedious lattice road.

(The King of Saxony's Journey thro' England and Scotland by his physician, DR C. G. CARUS, 1844)

To the author, the view from the site of Britannia Bridge along the Menai Strait to Thomas Telford's suspension bridge is one which gives absolute pleasure. Apparently, it was not so for Dr Carus (quoted above), but this demonstrates the subjectivity of beauty. Dr Carus went on to say: 'Other bridges, with their various arches and ornamental buttresses, may, and frequently do present objects of great beauty to the eye. This, however, is, and must always remain, a great mathematical figure'.

Indeed, the great mathematical figure approximates to a parabola but in the design of a long-span bridge structure dominates and its form should reflect this (The essence of an elegant bridge is simplicity of line, in which the structural form is expressed to the full) The addition of superfluous features will generally detract from the beauty of a bridge rather than enhance it. Brunel's design for the Clifton Bridge at Bristol (see Chapter 1) illustrates how simplicity of line immeasurably enriches the appearance of a bridge. In comparison, Telford's design for the Clifton Bridge (see Plate 18, p52) with its colossal Gothic-style piers clashes disastrously with the superb landscape of the Avon Gorge. As we shall see, the conservatism of Telford's design was probably influenced by damage to the Menai Suspension Bridge which was incurred in a gale a week after its opening for public use on 30 January 1826.

Proposals for crossing the Menai Strait date back to the beginning of the nineteenth century. Following the union of England and Ireland, a group of Irish MPs lobbied for improved communications between London and Dublin. This led to the appointment of John Rennie and Captain Joseph Huddart to report on an appropriate route and suitable further sites. They recommended Holyhead, access to which involved crossing the Menai Strait. Crossing the strait in a gale at night in a small sailing ferry was, to say the least, hazardous and the road between Shrewsbury and Holyhead (see Chapter 4) was in an appalling condition and described as 'a miserable tract composed of a succession of circuitous and craggy inequalities'. In 1801, John Rennie proposed a number of bridge designs for the Menai crossing which included the use of cast-iron arch ribs, but the government was involved in more pressing matters — the war against Napoleon. Rennie's bridge schemes were abandoned. John Rennie and others held the view that road building was not appropriate work for a civil engineer, but with the establishment of a Royal Mail coach service between Shrewsbury and Holyhead in 1808, there was further pressure to provide a less hazardous crossing of the Menai Strait. In 1810, Telford was commissioned by the government to report on the state of the roads from Shrewsbury and Chester to Holyhead and to submit proposals for bridging the Menai Strait. He submitted two designs: one consisting of three 260ft (79m) cast-iron arches separated by two 100ft (30m) span stone arches, the stone arches resisting the horizontal thrust of the iron arches; another consisted of a single cast-iron arch 500ft (152m) span with a rise of 100ft (30m) (see Fig 12). The method of constructing the arch ribs without support from

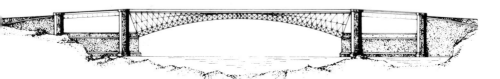

Fig 12 Telford's proposal of 1811 for spanning the Menai Strait with a single span cast-iron arch of 500ft (152m)

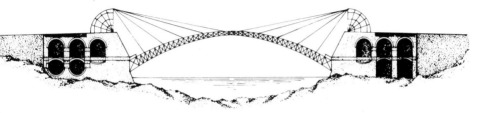

Fig 13 The method proposed by Telford for constructing the arch without support from below

below, which would have been difficult in the fast flowing water of the strait, is shown in Fig 13. A series of iron stays, 1½in (38mm) square, radiating from a timber tower was proposed. These stays could be tied back to the arch abutment and would remain in position until completion of erection of the arch ribs. Both designs were rejected by the Admiralty owing to the restricted headroom provided by the arch form.

In the interim period prior to the decision to construct a suspension bridge over the Menai Strait, Telford was able to develop his confidence in this form of construction through another impressive project, a suspension bridge across the River Mersey at Runcorn. Prior to considering Telford's work on the Runcorn project, the work of others on the development of suspension bridges will be briefly reviewed. In the Introduction, reference was made to James Finley's pioneering work in establishing the essential features of a suspension bridge and these were developed further by a captain in the Royal Navy, Samuel Brown. Brown was interested in the use of iron chains and rigging for ships (E. L. Kemp). Following his retirement from the Navy in 1812 he constructed a 105ft (32m) long model bridge in his factory at the Isle of Dogs. Brown and Telford came into contact over proposals to construct a bridge over the River Mersey at Runcorn Gap. Telford proposed a 2,000ft (612m) long bridge in 1814, but for financial reasons work did not proceed and by 1817 a number of other designs had been considered, including one by Brown. The two engineers conferred on technical aspects of suspension bridge design, but despite modifications to achieve economy, the project was abandoned in 1818. Telford went on to build the Menai Suspension Bridge and Brown became established as a leading bridge builder. He constructed the Union Bridge over the River Tweed in 1820, the first British suspension bridge to carry vehicular traffic with a span between towers of 437ft (133m). The deck spans 361ft (110m) and the bridge is in use today following reconstruction of the deck in 1974. Another well-known Brown design, the Brighton chain pier, was completed in 1823 with four 255ft (78m) spans. About ten years later it lost a span in a gale.

To return to Telford's design for the bridge at Runcorn, its significance is that it enabled Telford to undertake extensive experiments to establish the strength of wrought-iron bars. The 2,000ft (612m) overall span was to consist of a central suspension span of 1,000ft (306m) and two side suspension spans of 500ft (153m). Telford referred to the masonry towers as 'pyramids' (G. A. Maunsell) and the dip of the cables between the towers and the centre of the 1,000ft (306m) span was 50ft (15.3m). The ratio of the central span to the dip is thus 20, which is very high for a suspension bridge; a more realistic value would be between 10 and 12. It is shown in the Technical Appendix that if the cables were constructed to this flat curve, the stress in them under their own weight would be about $4T/in^2$ ($62N/mm^2$). It was fortuitous for Telford's reputation that this project was abandoned in 1818. It will be recalled (see Introduction) that in the competition for the Clifton Bridge, the stress in the chains resulting from the total weight of the bridge, plus traffic loading, was limited to $5\frac{1}{2}T/in^2$ ($85N/mm^2$).

In order to attempt to substantiate his design for the Runcorn bridge, Telford preferred the use of experimental methods rather than use theories proposed by mathematicians with 'minds half matured' (E. L. Kemp). In 1814, Telford carried out tests on 1in (25mm) square bars and 0.1in (2.5mm) diameter wires to establish the loads at which the iron would stretch (elastic limit) and break (ultimate tensile strength). Up to the elastic limit there is a linear relationship between the load applied and the extension of the bar/wire and on removal of the load it will return to its original length. If the load is increased beyond the elastic limit and then removed the bar/wire will not return to its original length: there is a permanent deformation. Telford established breaking limits of about $27T/in^2$ ($416N/mm^2$) and $40T/in^2$ ($616N/mm^2$) for the bars and wires respectively (R. A. Paxton). Designs using wire and bar cables were developed simultaneously, the square bars being butt welded together, 36 bars forming one cable.

Following the abandonment of the Runcorn bridge proposals, Telford reported to the Holyhead Road Commissioners on the feasibility of a suspension bridge over the Menai Strait and his scheme proposed the use of the bar cables referred to previously. The scheme was agreed and William Provis was appointed resident engineer in June 1818, and the foundation stone to the Anglesey pier was laid two months later. The masonry contractors were Stephen & Hall, but they resigned after less than a year's work. The work was let to John Wilson, one of Telford's masonry contractors on the Caledonian Canal, which was nearing completion (see Chapter 7). Work on the two 153ft (47m) high towers, the three approach arches on the Caernarvonshire side and the four on the Anglesey side fell behind schedule as a result of difficulties in transporting the limestone quarried near Penman Point on the south-east corner of Anglesey by ship to the site. Above the high-water mark, the towers are of cellular construction (Plate 49) and above the roadway level the stone blocks were dowelled together. The dowelling procedure is described by Maunsell:

Two holes about 1¼ in. diameter were drilled through every stone in every course and carried 6 in. into the course below. After these holes had been

Plate 49 The piers of Menai Bridge, of tapered (pyramid) form, are of cellular construction (*from* Telford's Atlas, *Richard Packer*)

bored, Parker or British cement mixed to a consistency similar to that which is used for pointing was put into each hole and wrought iron dowels 12 in. long and 1 in. (25mm) diameter were driven through the cement to the bottom of the drilled holes so that each dowel had a 6 in. grip in each of the adjacent courses of masonry. The cement completely filled the spaces around the dowels and the upper part of the holes was afterwards run full of grout before proceeding with the masonry course next above it.

The towers were not completed until 1824. The decision to change the cable design to eye bar links pinned together was made about four years previously. It was a wise decision as the need for extensive butt welding was eliminated. Telford may well have been influenced by the successful use of eye bar links by Samuel Brown in the construction of the chains for Union Bridge. Telford's design of 1818 was also modified as a result of an analysis of the chains by Davies Gilbert, who also advised on the Clifton Bridge (see Chapter 1). Gilbert was a member of the parliamentary committee responsible for the Menai bridge and it can be imagined that Telford was reluctant to take any 'theoretical' advice, but the towers were raised to increase the dip and thus the tension in the chains.

A further modification to the 1818 design was that instead of anchoring the cables into the approach viaducts, they were taken back to anchorage chambers beyond the viaducts. However, the vertical hangers were maintained (see Fig 5b, p22). Thus the bridge could have been built with suspended approach spans, as envisaged for the Runcorn Bridge.

The contract for the ironwork was awarded to William Hazledine in the summer of 1821. It was forged at Upton and then finished and tested at Shrewsbury. Each link or bar of the chains was of rectangular section 1in (25mm) × 3¼in (82mm), about 9ft 9in (3m) long with an eye at each end drilled to accept a 3in (75mm) diameter pin. At Shrewsbury, each link was tested to a load of 35 tons (350kN) in tension, just over 10T/in^2 (155N/mm^2) or twice the working stress of 5T/in^2 (78N/mm^2), which was eventually decided as being a safe value under the full load on the bridge. After each link was tested, it was cleaned, gently heated in a stove and immersed in a trough of linseed oil. On removal from the trough, it was put in the stove again to dry. When taken out of the stove again, a second coat of linseed oil was applied and allowed to dry.

The ironwork was transported by barge along the Ellesmere and Chester canals a distance of 54 miles (87km) to Chester (see Chapter 3) and then a further 60 miles (97km) to the site. A contemporary description of the erection of the chains taken from a Bill announcing their raising is given below, and the work was completed on 9 July 1825.

On Tuesday, the 26th April, 1825, the first Chain of this stupendous work was thrown over the Straits of Menai; the day was calm, and highly propitious for the purpose. An immense concourse of persons, of all ranks, began to assemble on the Anglesea and Carnarvonshire shores, about twelve o' clock at noon, to witness a scene, which our ancestors had never contemplated. Precisely at half past two o'clock, it being then about half-flood tide, the Raft, prepared for the occasion, stationed on the Carnarvonshire side, near Treborth Mill, which supported a part of the Chain intended to be drawn over, began to move gradually from its moorings, towed by four boats, with the assistance of the tide, in the centre of the river, between the two Grand Piers; when the Raft was properly adjusted, and brought to its ultimate situation, it was made fast to several buoys, anchored in the Channel for that specific purpose. The whole of this arduous process was accomplished in twenty-five minutes.

A part of the Chain, pending from the apex of the Suspending Pier, on the Carnarvonshire side, down nearly to high-water mark, was then made fast by a bolt, to that part of the Chain lying on the Raft, which operation was completed in ten minutes.

The next process was fastening the other extremity of the Chain (on the raft) to two immense powerful blocks, for the purpose of hoisting the entire line of Chain to its intended station, the apex of the Suspending Pier on the Anglesea side; the tension of the Chain then being 40 tons. When the blocks were made secure to the Chain, (comprising twenty-five ton weight of iron) two Capstans, and also two preventive Capstans, commenced working, each Capstan being propelled by thirty-two men.

To preserve an equanimity in the rotatory evolutions of the two principal Capstans, two fifers played several enlivening tunes, to keep the men regular in their steps, for which purpose they had been previously trained.

At this critical and interesting juncture, the attention of the numberless spectators, assembled on the occasion, seemed rivetted to the novel spectacle, now presented to their anxious view; the Chain rose majestically, and the gratifying sight was enthusiastically enjoyed by each individual present.

At fifty minutes after four o'clock, the final bolt was fixed, which completed the whole line of Chain, and the happy event was hailed by the hearty acclamations of the numerous spectators, joined by the vociferations of the workmen, which had a beautiful effect from the reiteration of sound, caused by the heights of the opposite banks of the river. Not the least accident, delay, or failure in any department, took place during the whole operation, which does infinite credit to every individual employed in this grand work.

From the casting off of the Raft, to the uniting of the Chain, took up only two hours and twenty minutes, which appears truly astonishing, when the magnitude of the work is considered, and which could only be appreciated by those who had an opportunity of viewing it — a work, differing, in design, from every other Bridge, and which, undeniably, has not its equal in the world.

This National, and splendid specimen of British Architecture, will be a lasting monument to the discernment of the present Government, for having called into requisition, the transcendent talents of Mr. TELFORD, (who was present on the occasion) who has thus proved himself, in this line, the first Architect of the age.

The masterly manner in which the various concomitant parts of this magnificent Bridge have been executed, will remain an indelible proof of the superior abilities of Mr. William Alexander Provis, the resident Engineer; Mr. John Wilson, the Contractor of the Masonry; Mr. Hazledine, the Ironfounder, Shrewsbury; and Mr. Thomas Rhodes, the superintendent Engineer of the Iron and Timber work.

Upon the completion of the Chain, three of the workmen, viz. H. Davis, stone-mason, M. Williams, labourer, and John Williams, carpenter, had the temerity to pass along the upper surface of the chain, which forms a curvature of 590 feet. The versed sine of the arch is 43 feet.

On the termination of the day's proceedings, each workman (about 150 in number) was regaled, by order of the Right Hon the Parliamentary Commissioners of the Holyhead Road Improvements, with a quart of 'Cwrw da'.

The following is a summary account of the Dimensions of the Bridge: The extreme length of the Chain, from the fastenings in the Rocks, is about 1714 feet. The height of the road-way, from high water line, is 100 feet. Each of the seven small Piers, from high water line to the spring of the arches, is 65 feet. The span of each arch is 52 feet. Each of the two Suspending Piers is 52 feet above the road. The road on the Bridge consists of two carriage-ways, of 12 feet each, with a foot-path of four feet, in the centre. The length of the suspended part of the road, from Pier to Pier, is 553 feet. The carriage roads pass through two arches, in the Suspending Piers, of the width of nine feet, by fifteen feet in height to the spring of the arches. To counteract the contraction and expansion of the iron, from the effect of the change of the atmosphere in Winter and Summer, a set of Rollers are placed under cast-iron saddles, on top of the Suspending Piers, where the Chains rest. The vertical rods, an inch square, suspended from the Chains, support the sleepers for the flooring of the road-way, the rods being placed five feet from each other. The Chains, sixteen in number, consist of five bars each; length of the bar nine feet nine inches, width three inches by one inch — with six connecting lengths at each joint, one foot six inches, by ten inches, and one inch — secured by two bolts at each joint, each bolt weighing about 56 pounds, and the total number of bars, in the cross section of the Chains, is 80.

Menai Bridge was finally opened for public use on 30 January 1826, taking about eight years to construct, and at this time was easily the largest clear span in the world. Unfortunately, Telford was not able to relax, as a week after the opening a gale damaged the timber deck (Plate 50) and some of the 1in (25mm) square hangers broke. Some strengthening was carried out but undulation of the deck was a continuing cause for concern and in 1836 the bridge-master observed vertical oscillations of 'a little less than 16 ft' (5m) (R. A. Paxton, G. A. Maunsell). The immediate reaction is that there was some (!) exaggeration; nevertheless, a substantial part of the deck was destroyed during a storm in 1839. The deck was redesigned by William Provis and the repair work was completed in 1840 at about 5 per cent of the capital cost of the bridge — £178,000. Provis's timber deck, which weighed 130 tons (1300kN) more than the original, was replaced in 1893 by a steel deck

Transverse Section through the Main Chains and Roadway

Carriage Way

Foot Path

Carriage Way

Oak Guards

Oak Guards

Plan of Roadway Bars

which was designed by Sir Benjamin Baker. It is of interest to note that in 1839 George Stephenson proposed to lay a single-track railway on one carriageway and horses were to be used to draw the trains across. In view of the previous history of movement of the deck, it is surprising that Stephenson considered that the additional loading could be accepted.

In the 1920s, a series of investigations led to the installation of weighbridges at each end of the bridge (G. A. Maunsell) and vehicle weights were restricted to 4½ tons (45kN). The speed limit of vehicles on crossing the bridge was 4mph (6.4km/h) and they had to maintain 50ft (15.3m) intervals.

Between 1938 and 1941 the deck and chains were replaced to the design of Sir Alexander Gibb & Partners. The bridge was by then under the control of the Ministry of Transport and the Ministry's requirements included the provision of a dual carriageway and two 5ft (1.5m) wide footways and, most important, the appearance of the bridge should be maintained as far as possible. Fortunately, it was not necessary to alter the appearance of the approach arches and the towers significantly. Plate 51 shows the dual carriageway and the footways. It was necessary to increase the width of the openings in the towers by 12in (300mm) and to corbel out on each side of the approach arches to accommodate the footways. It should be noted that two sets of chains, one pair on each side of the deck, replaced the four sets of chains, four chains in each set, on the original bridge.

It can be seen from Plate 52 that Sir Alexander Gibb & Partners successfully retained the original appearance of the bridge, including the redundant vertical hangers from the chains to the approach viaducts, and the following description by Mr John Smith in his *Guide to Snowdonia* (*Wanderings through North Wales by Thomas Roscoe 1836*) is still relevant:

Having landed, by means of boats, upon the Anglesey side, we proceeded to the bridge, the visiting of which is a new era in the lives of those who have not

Plate 50 A section through the original deck showing the light timber deck and the 1in square hangers (*from* Telford's Atlas, *Richard Packer*)

Plate 51 (*overleaf inset*) Although the original chains and hangers were replaced in 1940, this view taken in 1984 shows the vertical hangers connecting the chains to the approach viaducts. Though not structurally necessary, the hangers maintain the original appearance of the bridge (*Derrick Beckett*)

Plate 52 (*main picture*) This view of the Menai Bridge, taken from the Caernarvon bank, demonstrates the elegance of Telford's great work (*Derrick Beckett*)

Plate 53 Conwy Suspension Bridge, a view looking along the deck from the Conwy Castle abutment looking east. Note Robert Stephenson's tubular bridge to the right incorporates castellations in the abutment, as with Telford's bridge, reflecting the architecture of Conwy Castle (*Derrick Beckett*)

before had the pleasure, and is a renewed luxury to those who have seen it again and again. Our party walked over the bridge slowly, because there was something to be admired at every step: — the effect of a passing carriage; the vibration caused even by a hand applied to the suspending rods; the depth to the level of the water; the fine view of the Straits in both directions; the lofty pillar erected in honour of Lord Anglesey; the diminutive appearance of persons on the shore; the excellence and strength of the workmanship; the beauty of the arches over the road through the suspension piers, and the echo in them, — all conspired to delight and to detain us. Many of our party went down the steep bank to the foot of the bridge, from which point, certainly, the best view is to be had of the whole structure, inasmuch as by being in contact, as it were, with its proportions on terra firma, a better idea can be formed of its real, and indeed, wonderful dimensions. We actually lingered about the spot, careless of time, or of aught but the scene we were contemplating. There is so much magnificence, beauty, and elegance in this grand work of art, that it harmonises and accords perfectly with the natural scenery around, and though itself an object of admiration, still in connexion it heightens the effect of the general view.

Six months after the opening of the Menai Suspension Bridge, a smaller but visually appealing suspension bridge carrying the Chester to Holyhead road over the Conwy estuary was opened to public traffic. The foundation stone was laid in April 1822 and it took just over four years to build. The distance between the two supporting towers is 327ft (100m). Plate 53 was taken from the Conwy Castle abutment looking east (see also Plate 83, p166). It is now a pedestrian bridge but 150 years ago mail coaches could be seen thundering across it en route to the Menai Bridge and Holyhead.

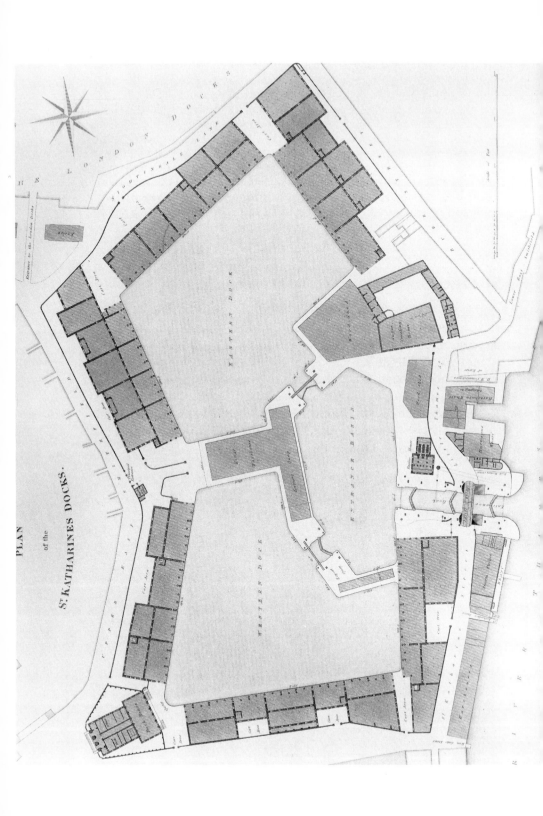

PLAN

of the

St KATHARINE'S DOCKS.

6
ST KATHARINE DOCKS

Seldom, indeed, never within my knowledge, has there been an in-
stance of an undertaking of this magnitude, in a very confined situation,
having been perfected in so short a time . . . but as a practical engineer,
responsible for the success of difficult operations, I must be allowed to
protest against such haste, pregnant as it was, and ever will be, with
risks, which, in more instances than one, severely taxed all my experi-
ence and skill, and dangerously involved the reputation of the directors
as well as their engineer.

(THOMAS TELFORD)

Telford was referring to the construction of St Katharine Docks, one of
a number of important docks built in the Port of London between 1800
and 1834. By 1800, trade on the River Thames at London had increased
to a level at which loading and unloading at riverside wharves, restricted
by tides, became impractical. The construction of docks with locks to
maintain water at a constant level facilitated loading and unloading and
further it was easier to maintain security, pilfering being rife at the time.

The St Katharine Docks Company was formed in 1824 and the site
chosen was close to the centre of London, a short distance downstream
from the Tower on the north bank of the river. The 23 acre (9.5 hectares) site was heavily populated and it was necessary to demolish over
1,200 dwellings, which displaced over 11,000 inhabitants. The hospital
of St Katharine was also demolished, but was found a new site.

Telford had extensive previous experience of dock and harbour work
obtained over a period in excess of twenty years, including the Caledonian Canal (Chapter 7), and Aberdeen Harbour (Chapter 1). This no
doubt led to his engagement by the Dock Company to draw up a preliminary scheme in conjunction with the architect, Philip Hardwick
(1792–1870). It must be remembered that at the time of his appointment by the Dock Company, Telford was heavily involved with the
construction of the Menai Suspension Bridge (Chapter 5). Fees of £291
and £259 respectively were paid to Telford and Hardwick for this preliminary work and a further £125 was expended on borings to establish

Plate 54 The plan of St Katharine Docks, showing the entrance basin and the eastern
and western docks (*from* Telford's Atlas, *Richard Packer*)

ENTRANCE LOCK.

Longitudinal Section.

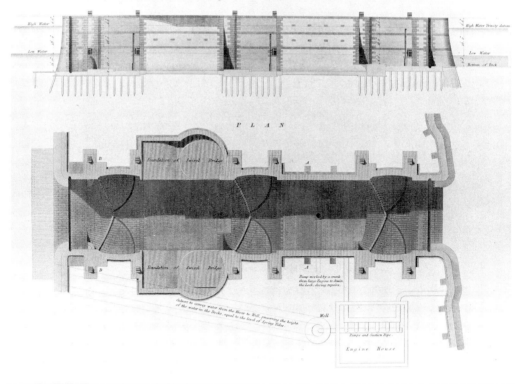

CAST IRON SWIVEL BRIDGE over the ENTRANCE LOCK.

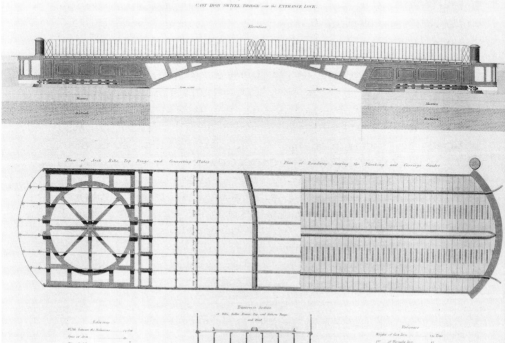

the ground conditions (A. W. Skempton). Their official appointments, both at salaries of £500 per annum, came shortly after the Act for building the docks, which was obtained in June 1825. The plan of the docks (see Plate 54, from *Telford's Atlas*) is unusual in that the 10½ acre (4.2 hectares) water area is in three parts: the entrance basin, the eastern dock and western dock. This arrangement enabled the maximum length of warehousing and quay to be constructed. The two docks were isolated from the entrance basin by a single pair of gates and thus the water level could be maintained constant if that in the entrance basin fluctuated. Telford indicated that one dock could be emptied for cleaning and repair while the other remained in use. It can be seen from the plan that the mitred gates point the wrong way and in fact they were never drained, and silt was removed by dredging (M. Tucker). Entrance to the 1¾ acre (0.7 hectares) basin from the river required the construction of a massive entrance lock 45ft (13.7m) wide and 180ft (54.8m) long. Plate 55, (*Telford's Atlas*) shows a plan and longitudinal section of the dock and it should be noted that a central pair of gates was fitted. Their purpose was to allow small vessels to pass through the lock using half the volume of water. The plan also shows the foundations to a cast-iron swing bridge, details of which are shown in Plate 56. Two Boulton & Watt steam engines were installed (see bottom right-hand corner of the plan) to pump water from the river via a culvert into the basin or lock chamber. This meant that the water level in the lock could be raised quickly, about 12ft (3.7m) in 5½ minutes (M. Tucker). In order to construct the entrance lock it was necessary to erect a timber cofferdam, 207ft (63m) long. Work on the cofferdam commenced in the summer of 1826 supervised by Thomas Rhodes, the resident engineer, who had previously assisted Telford on the Menai Suspension Bridge. The cofferdam acted as a massive watertight wall which allowed excavation of the lock chamber to proceed behind it. The sill level (see Introduction) at the river end of the lock chamber was 28ft (8.5m) below Trinity High Water, which represented the high-water level of ordinary spring tides. The specification for the construction of the cofferdam was published in the *Civil Engineer and Architects' Journal*, November 1839 (E. Dobson), on which the following simplified description is based. Reference should be made to Fig 14, which shows a section through the completed cofferdam.

Plate 55 Details of the entrance lock (*from* Telford's Atlas, *Richard Packer*)

Plate 56 The cast-iron swing bridge over the entrance lock (*from* Telford's Atlas, *Richard Packer*)

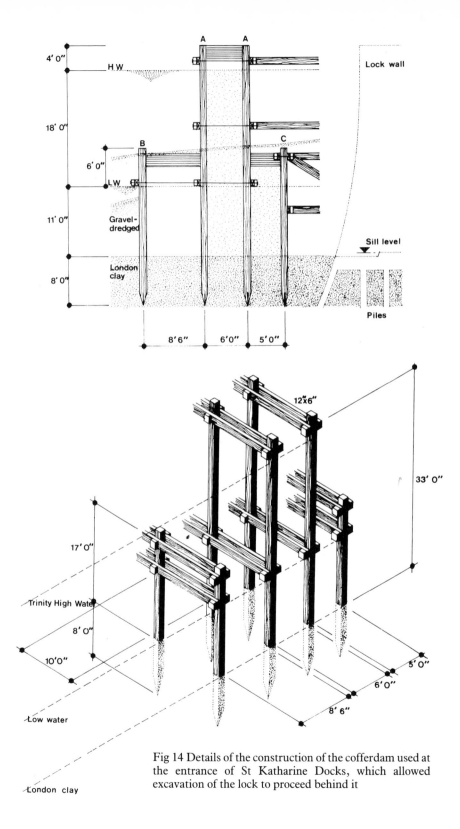

Fig 14 Details of the construction of the cofferdam used at the entrance of St Katharine Docks, which allowed excavation of the lock to proceed behind it

The central section of the cofferdam was made up of two rows of timber piles, 6ft (1.8m) apart and 12in (300mm) square (A) which were driven 8ft (2.4m) below the level of the bottom of the lock into the blue London clay. Before this could be achieved it was necessary to dredge out the gravel to the level of the clay. Additional rows of piles B and C were driven into the clay to strengthen the lower portion of the cofferdam. Piles A, B and C were driven at 10ft (3.06m) intervals along the length of the wall. These are known as gauge piles. Two rows of temporary double timbers (walings), 12in × 6in (300mm × 150mm) were then bolted to the gauge piles at approximately high- and low-water levels.

The space between the gauge piles was filled by driving further piles between the gap in the walings. After this had been completed, the temporary walings were replaced by permanent ones. These are shown in Fig 14 together with 2in (50mm) diameter tie bolts which were at 5ft (1.53m) centres.

The construction of this massive wall required over 800 piles to be driven into the London clay. The method used was to subject the top of the pile to a series of blows by means of an iron block (monkey) which was raised by a pulley to the top of a timber frame. The block was allowed to fall freely between timber guides on to the top of the pile. In order to prevent the tops of the piles splitting under the impact, they were capped with wrought-iron shoes and bound with iron hoofs. A number of 'pile engines', as they were called, were in use simultaneously as it took about a day to drive one pile to the correct level. The term 'pile engine' is misleading as it could imply the use of steam power. The steam hammer invented by William Nasmyth (1808–90) was a later development and used to great effect in the construction of the cofferdam for the High Level Bridge at Newcastle (see *Stephensons' Britain*). The use of steam power reduced the time to drive a single pile to a few minutes. Steam engines were, however, used to pump water out of the spaces between the rows of piles forming the cofferdam. The spaces were then filled with clay, but the upper part of the central portion between pile lines A was finished with bricks bedded on sand. This prevented the clay from drying out and shrinking. The timbers running out to the right of pile line C were used to brace the cofferdam against the lock walls as they were built up.

Excavation of the gravel and sand to form the basin and the two docks was a monumental task. Extensive use was made of horse-drawn waggons on railways and steam power was employed to haul waggons up inclined planes. The excavated material was transported upstream by barge to Chelsea for use in land reclamation. Although it was necessary to construct the dock walls in the dry, a further problem was to prevent

Plate 57 Cast-iron columns on the north side of the western dock (subsequently removed) (*Derrick Beckett*)

Plate 58 A view looking along the entrance lock towards Ivory House. Note the Italianate campanile (*Derrick Beckett*)

the water contained within the docks draining away through the gravel layer above the clay (see Fig 14). The dock floors were sealed with puddled clay and this was also placed behind the walls. The gravel below the dock walls was sealed by driving sheet piles into the London clay below, effectively cutting off the flow of water. During the construction of the quay walls round the perimeter of the excavations, it is likely that both steam and horse-powered pumps were employed to control the entry of water. The brick quay walls are 33ft (10m) high, 10ft (3.06m) wide at the base and reducing to 5ft 3in (1.6m) at the top. The stone blocks for the top course of the quay walls were quarried near Leeds and transported by canal and sea. Each block weighed about 1½ tons (15kN). The tops of the quay walls are chamfered at a number of locations to accommodate the bowsprits of sailing ships.

Philip Hardwick designed the warehouses to extend along three sides of each dock, east and west. Thus there were six warehouses in all and they were constructed between 1827 and 1830. An interesting feature is that they were built up to the edge of the quays and supported by hollow cast-iron columns 16ft 9in (5.1m) high at 18ft (5.5m) centres. This series of columns with entablatures (Doric order) formed an impressive colonnade (see Plate 57). The brick external walls above the colonnades extended to a height of about 80ft (24m) above the quay level. The slate-clad timber roof trusses were masked by a parapet and internally the wooden floors were supported by cast-iron columns of cruciform section (M. Tucker) (see Longdon on Tern Aqueduct, p159). Unfortunately, it has not been possible to retain any of Hardwick's warehouses in the redevelopment scheme (see later). The warehouse on the quay separating the east and west docks, Ivory House (Plate 58), was designed by one of Hardwick's contemporaries, George Aicheson. It remains substantially as built, including the Italianate campanile (bell tower). In the 1850s the bell rang at 6am to wake the dockers who commenced work at 7am and earned the equivalent of 1½ new pence an hour. The warehouse was used exclusively for exports and derives its name from extensive trade with the Ivory Coast. It now has a multi-purpose use: a yacht club, apartments, shops and a restaurant.

The 850 bedroom Tower Hotel on the south side of the site between the entrance lock and Tower Bridge approach was the site of warehouse A. As with warehouses B and C, it was used to store raw materials from all over the world, including cotton, silks, furs, hardwoods, spices and carpets. Warehouse B was a massive structure about 470ft (144m) long built at right-angles to warehouse A running parallel to St Katharine's Way (see Gazetteer, p157). It is now the site of International House, an eight-storey brick-faced reinforced concrete framed structure which retains features of Hardwick's warehouse, including the quayside Doric columns and dockside cranes.

The World Trade Centre, currently being extended, is on the site of warehouse C, which was built along the north side of the west dock.

In a similar manner, warehouses D, E and F were built round the east dock. Again, they handled a wide range of goods, exports and imports to and from all parts of the world. The warehouses had the advantage of being within easy carting distance from the London railway termini.

The first ship entered the docks on 25 October 1828, which marked the formal opening of the basin and the west dock warehouses A, B and C. The eastern dock was opened in the autumn of 1829 and warehouses D, E and F a year later, the total cost being in the order of £250,000, including property purchase. In 1830, about 900 ships used the docks with a total tonnage in excess of 140,000. Vessels of over 600 tons were able to use the docks, but it was necessary to dredge the approach channel out to the centre of the river in order that the larger vessels could enter the lock and basin. Ships using the two docks were unaffected by changes in water level as stop locks were provided at each entrance.

Telford's involvement with the construction ceased in the summer of 1830, and Hardwick's shortly after. Credit must be given to the contractor, George Burge. He was unable to commence work on excavation for the entrance lock, basin and western dock until May 1826. The cofferdam, as we have seen, was a massive undertaking involving several months of work. The labour force was reputed to have exceeded 1,000 and it is a tribute to all involved that the docks were opened less than 2½ years after commencement of excavations. Further, the docks have remained substantially watertight to this day.

By 1835, nine London docks were handling a tonnage of approximately one million, but regrettably could not be adapted to mechanised handling, nor could they accommodate the increasing size of ships and thus, inevitably, St Katharine Docks were closed in 1968. The Greater London Council purchased the freehold from the Port of London Authority for £1.8 million in 1969. Following an open competition, St Katharine-by-the-Tower Ltd, a member of the Taylor Woodrow Group, was granted a franchise to develop the site. This area of London is a haven for tourists — the Tower of London, Tower Bridge and St Katharine Docks. The annual number of visitors to the docks is in excess of two million. The most interesting feature is the continuing use of the basin and the two docks by a variety of craft. However, the sight of a glass fibre hulled cabin cruiser entering the basin has not the same romance as the four-master sailing ship, *Augustus Ceasar* (Captain Crocker), arriving from Australia some 150 years ago.

7

THE CALEDONIAN CANAL

Where these capacious basins, by the laws of the adjacent element, receive
The Ship, descending or upraised eight times,
From stage to stage with unfelt agency
Translated, fitliest may the marble here
Record the Architect's immortal name.
TELFORD *it was by whose presiding mind*
The whole great work was planned and perfected, . . .

(ROBERT SOUTHEY)

Robert Southey's lines, inscribed on a marble slab outside the British Waterways Board's Canal Office at Clachnaharry, near Inverness, are a tribute to Thomas Telford's work in the planning and supervision of the construction of the Caledonian Canal through the Great Glen to link the east to the west coast of Scotland. The highland region of Scotland is all but severed between the Moray Firth and the Firth of Lorn by a series of sea- and fresh-water lochs running in a direction north-east to south-west. This quirk of nature invited a number of proposals for a complete waterway which required the construction of twenty miles of artificial canal.

As we have seen (see Introduction) there was extensive engineering activity of a military nature in the Great Glen between 1725 and 1736, and the military road system was extended until the 1780s; it comprised nearly 700 miles of road and about 1,000 bridges. However, the military road network did little to alleviate social distress in the Highlands and there was extensive emigration.

Following a survey of the Highlands by John Knox in 1784, two societies were formed: the Highland Society and the British Fisheries Society, with the aim of improving communications and the employment situation. Sir William Pulteney was a founder member of the British Fisheries Society and thus Telford was appointed as engineer to the society.

In July 1801, Telford was instructed by the Treasury to carry out a survey of the Highlands and his brief included the selection of appropriate sites for fishing stations on the west coast, to plan improvements in communications by road and to investigate the possibility of constructing a canal through the Great Glen. Prior to submitting his report, Telford consulted James Watt (1736–1819).

In 1773, Watt was instructed by the Commissioners of the Forfeited Estates to survey a route for the canal; his estimate for a channel 10ft deep with 32 locks was £164,000. John Rennie (1761–1821) also consulted James Watt in 1793 on a further proposal which was abandoned. Telford's report, which was completed by the end of November 1801, convinced the Treasury of the viability of a canal.

In the summer of 1802, Telford was instructed by the Treasury to undertake a more detailed survey, which was of course backed by the influential Highland Society and British Fisheries Society. Detailed plans were prepared and the estimated cost was about £350,000, with a construction time of seven years. This proposal was considered by a Parliamentary Select Committee with Jessop and Rennie giving evidence. Jessop reported that 'under the favourable circumstances of ground tolerably even, and the soil moderately good, I should suppose it might cost about £2,000 a mile including locks, bridges and canal and other necessary works making no allowance for any extra works'.

The Select Committee was satisfied of the feasibility of the project and a preliminary Act was passed in July 1803. A Board of Commissioners was set up, which included amongst its staff John Rickman (secretary), Thomas Telford (engineer) and William Jessop (consultant). Jessop played an important part in the early stages of work on the canal and apparently Telford was happy with this arrangement. Jessop did not visit Scotland until October 1803, but some preparatory work on the canal had already been carried out under Telford's direction. Jessop proceeded with his own survey and this was followed by a report in January 1804, which gave a figure of £417, 531 for the construction of the canal excluding land costs. In June 1804 Jessop put this figure to the Lords Committee on the second Caledonian Bill and Telford provided the estimate for the cost of land to be purchased, which amounted to £15,000.

Between 1804 and 1812, Jessop and Telford worked closely on all aspects of work on the canal, with Jessop as the first signatory on reports prepared for the Commissioners. By 1812, Jessop's health was deteriorating and his last visit with Telford to the canal was in October of that year. He died in November 1814 and Telford was left on his own to see the work through to completion.

To return to the reasons for building the Caledonian Canal, these were both strategic and commercial. Prior to the development of steamships, sailing ships encountered great difficulties in navigating between the North Sea and the Atlantic via the Pentland Firth, between the north coast of Scotland and the Orkney Islands, and the aptly named Cape Wrath. With the construction of a canal this treacherous sea passage could be avoided. It must be remembered that at the beginning of the nineteenth century bulk transport of materials by ship between the west and east coasts of Britain was extensive, as the roads were completely inadequate for transportation of heavy goods. Additionally, there was a significant timber trade between the western coats of Britain and the Baltic.

Further, Britain was at war with France and a canal would serve to protect merchant ships and provide a strategic route for ships at war. In 1804, Jessop and Telford reported that at a small additional cost, 32 gun frigates could be accommodated and thus the Board of Commissioners decided to increase the size of the locks accordingly. As built, the sizes of the locks vary and can take ships of the following dimensions: 160ft (48.77m) long × 35ft (10.67m) beam × 9ft (2.67m) draught of 150ft (45.72m) long × 35ft (10.67m) beam × 13.5ft (4.11m) draught.

Telford and Jessop proposed that the lock chambers should be 170ft (52.3m) long by 40ft (12.3m) wide and the canal dimensions 110ft (33.8m) wide at the top, 50ft (15.4m) wide at the bottom and 20ft (6.15m) deep. An approximate cross section through the Caledonian Canal is shown in Fig 15 and compared with that of the Ellesmere Canal (see Chapter 3), shown dotted. Although the dimensions of the Caledonian Canal dwarf those of the Ellesmere Canal, which was nearing completion at the time the second Caledonian Bill was passed, they were still not adequate to cope with the rapid increase in the size of shipping. Further, the development of steam-powered vessels (see *Brunel's Britain*) meant that the sea passage through the Pentland Firth became

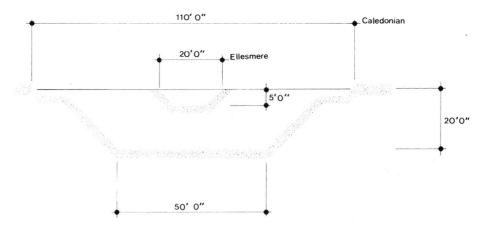

Fig 15 A comparison of the cross sections of the Caledonian and Ellesmere Canals

less onerous. The canal was opened for through passage on 23 October 1822 at a cost of £912,375.00 — far in excess of the 1804 estimate. Unfortunately, there were a number of shortcomings in the construction which led to its closure for extensive repair works, in particular to the locks. The repair work was carried out between 1843 and 1847 and the canal was re-opened on 1 May 1847 with a total cost to that date of £1,262,005.00. In 1920 the Ministry of Transport took over responsibility for the canal from the Commissioners and in 1948 this responsibility was transferred to the British Transport Commission.

As a result of the Transport Act of 1962 the canal is now administered by the British Waterways Board, and lock mechanisation was completed in 1968.

The Caledonian Canal is the earliest example of nationalised transport in Britain. Although still used by fishing vessels, the canal was never commercially successful, but has immense potential as a tourist attraction. As a result of a movement of the earth's crust on a fault line over 250 million years ago, nature has provided the greater part of this spectactular waterway, which includes the 22 mile (36km) long Loch Ness, with the attraction of 'Nessie'. Along the canal there has been extensive conifer planting on the waterside slopes and this contrasts with the bare mountainside above. At Banavie the canal is overlooked by the highest mountain in the British Isles — Ben Nevis, 4,406ft (1,343m). The contribution of man to this 60 mile (97km) long waterway — 20

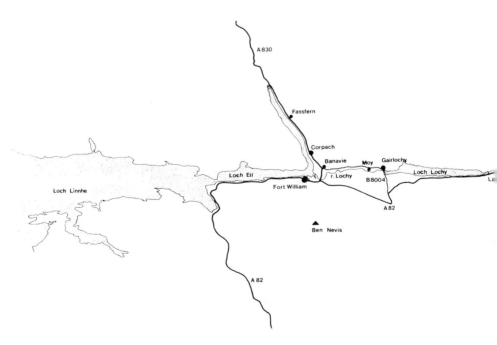

miles (32km) of artificial canal — is an outstanding example of working industrial archaeology, and the civil engineering and organisational aspects of the work leading up to its completion will now be described.

By any standards the Caledonian Canal was an immense project and the construction problems were exacerbated by its remoteness and poor communications. The route of the canal is shown in Fig 16, and it should be noted that the locks are all above sea level and at different levels:

Loch Lochy   96ft (29.4m) above sea level
Loch Oich   106ft (32.4m) above sea level
Loch Ness   52ft (15.9m) above sea level

The summit is Loch Oich, and thus it was necessary to construct a number of locks, as listed in Table 4.

Table 4   The locks of the Caledonian Canal

	No. of locks		No. of locks
Clachnaharry (sea lock)	1	Cullochy	1
Clachnaharry (works lock)	1	Laggan	2
Muirtown	4	Gairlochy	2
Dochgarroch	1	Banavie (Neptune's Staircase)	8
Fort Augustus	5	Corpach basin	3
Kytra	1		—
		Total	29
			—

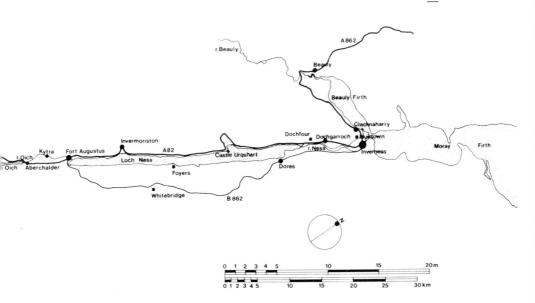

Fig 16 The route of the Caledonian Canal between Fort William and Inverness

At the Fort William end, the canal commences with a tidal sea lock at Corpach at the junction of Loch Eil and Loch Linnhe. The sea lock was lengthened in the 1960s, allowing larger ships to enter Corpach to unload timber for the pulp mill, but the mill was closed in 1980. At the other end of the basin there are two locks which raise the level of the vessels to the section of the canal extending to the village of Banavie. In this section the canal is crossed by the road to the Isles (A830, see Chapter 8) and the West Highland Railway, which passes through Glenfinnan and Arisaig en route to Mallaig. At Banavie the canal rises 64ft (19.6m) via a flight of eight locks known as 'Neptune's Staircase': see Plate 59, which is a view taken from the bottom of the flight. The lock-keepers' houses are listed buildings (Plate 60) and closely resemble Telford's designs for toll-houses on the London to Holyhead road (see Chapter 4). Between Banavie and Gairlochy the canal follows the route of the River Lochy but at a higher level (see Plate 61). This view was taken from the B8004 close to Gairlochy and looking towards Gairlochy. The double-leaf form access swing bridge at Moy is the only original bridge structure crossing

the canal and is constructed of cast iron. A joint decision was made by Telford and Jessop to use cast iron for the eight bridges between Banavie and Inverness, and the design was based on the swing bridges constructed in the West India Docks, Poplar, which were opened in 1802. William Jessop was the engineer. Moy bridge is opened by means of a capstan which swings one half horizontally to the side of the canal. It is then necessary to cross to the other side of the canal by means of a dinghy to repeat the procedure. The ironwork for Moy bridge was cast at William Hazledine's foundry at Plas Kynaston. The remaining bridges carrying roads across the canal were replaced in the 1930s.

At Gairlochy there are two locks, the upper lock being added in 1844. Above the upper lock there is a picturesque basin which leads into Loch Lochy (see Plates 62 and 63). Two further locks were required at Laggan to raise the canal to its summit at a height of 106ft (32.4m) above sea

Plate 59 Looking up the flight of eight locks known as 'Neptune's Staircase', at Banavie (*Derrick Beckett*); (*inset*) Plate 60 The lock-keepers' houses closely resemble Telford's toll-house designs on the London to Holyhead road (*Derrick Beckett*)

Plate 61 Looking down onto the Caledonian Canal with the River Lochy below (taken from the B8004) *(Derrick Beckett)*

level. The link between Loch Lochy and Loch Oich required a massive cutting, which was vividly described by Robert Southey, the Poet Laureate who kept a journal of his tour of Scotland in 1819 accompanied by Telford and John Rickman.

We walked along the works between the Lakes Oich and Lochy. Here the lakes are what they call 'at deep cutting', this being the highest approach in the line, the Oich flowing to the East, the Lochy to the Western sea. This part is performed under contract by Mr. Wilson, a Cumberland man from Dalston, under the superintendence of Mr. Easton, the resident Engineer. And here also a Lock is building. The earth is removed by horses walking along the bench of the Canal, and drawing the laden cartlets up one inclined plane, while the emptied ones, which are connected with them by a chain passing over pullies, are let down another. This was going on in numberless places, and such a mass of earth had been thrown up on both sides along the whole line, that the men appeared in the proportion of emmets to an ant-hill, amid their own work. The hour of rest for men and horses is announced by blowing a horn; and so well have the horses learnt to measure time by their own exertions and sense of fatigue, that if the signal be delayed by five minutes, they stop of their own accord, without it.

This technique of excavating large volumes of material was subsequently used extensively by railway engineers (see *Stephensons' Britain*: the London & Birmingham Railway).

Loch Oich required extensive dredging to deepen the navigable channel through it, which is marked by buoys and beacons. The work was facilitated by the employment of steam bucket dredgers, and to quote Southey: '. . . at this end of Loch Oich a dredging machine is employed which brings up 800 tons a day'. The steam dredgers used at Loch Oich and again at Fort Augustus were among the first to be used and were constructed at Bryan Donkins' Butterley Ironworks. The use of a chain fitted with buckets for the purpose of raising water has been known for about 2,000 years and the first application for dredging purposes was at the end of the sixteenth century. Power was by means of a horse mill. When the resistance to movement of the chain became too high, the horse stopped, but with the development of steam power it was necessary to provide an easily replaceable component which would fail at a given load. A dredger of this type was designed by Jessop in 1806 and it was used for the deepening of Aberdeen harbour in 1811. A modified version was employed on the Caledonian Canal.

In order to bring the canal to the level of Loch Ness, single locks were built at Cullochy and Kytra and a staircase of five locks at Fort Augustus. The chamber of the bottom lock at Fort Augustus had to be excavated to a level below that of Loch Ness. It was founded on permeable

Plate 62 The basin above the upper loch at Gairlochy (*Derrick Beckett*)

Plate 63 A view from the basin looking towards Loch Lochy. Note the lighthouse reflected in the water (*Derrick Beckett*)

strata which resulted in a massive flow of water into the chamber. In order to control the flow of water it was necessary to install all the Boulton & Watt pumping engines used in the construction of the canal. A side wall of the bottom lock eventually failed, necessitating part of the repair work described previously.

The engineering works at Fort Augustus are again described by Robert Southey:

Went before breakfast to look at the Locks, five together, of which three are finished, the fourth about half-built, the fifth not quite excavated. Such an extent of masonry, upon such a scale, I have never before beheld, each of these Locks being 180 feet in length. It was a most impressive and rememberable scene. Men, horses and machines at work; digging, walling and puddling going on, men wheeling barrows, horses drawing stones along the railways. The great steam engine was at rest, having done its work. It threw out 160 hogsheads per minute; and two smaller engines were also needed while the excavation of the lower locks was going on; for they dug 24 feet below the surface of water . . . and the water filtered thro' open gravel. The dredging machine was in action, revolving round and round, and bringing up at every turn matter which had never before been brought to the air and light. Its chimney poured forth volumes of black smoke, which there was no annoyance in beholding, because there was room enough for it in this wide clear atmosphere. The iron for a pair of lockgates was lying on the ground, having just arrived from Derbyshire: the same vessel in which it was shipt at Gainsborough, landed it here at Fort Augustus. To one like myself not practically conversant with machinery, it seemed curious to hear Mr. Telford talk of the propriety of weighing these enormous pieces and to hear Cargill reply that it was easily done.

Fort Augustus is approximately halfway between Fort William and Inverness and the following 22 miles (35.6km) of the route were provided by nature in the form of Loch Ness. There were no depth problems here: it is in fact deeper than the North Sea, generally 600 to 700ft (183 to 215m) and near Urquhart Castle up to 1,000ft (308m). The problem with Loch Ness was the headwinds which caused conditions as

rough as at sea, thus impeding the passage of sailing ships. At the
northern end of Loch Ness there is a further small loch (Loch Dochfour).
Between Loch Dochfour and the approaches to Inverness the canal and
the River Ness run in parallel, and there is a regulatory lock at Dochgarroch
which prevents changes in water level in the loch affecting the water
level in the canal.

There was extensive leakage on this section of the canal and the repair
was effected by placing woollen cloth on the bed and sides of the
emptied channel. On top of this were placed several layers of puddle
(see p16). The canal enters Muirtown Basin via a flight of four locks (see
Plate 64). The basin at Muirtown, which is 2,400ft (734m) long and
420ft (128m) wide, was excavated to provide Inverness with a second
harbour. Plate 65 gives an indication of the size of the basin with a lock
gate lifting-boat moored in readiness. The penultimate lock (works
lock) is at the north end of Muirtown Basin adjacent to the canal village
of Clachnaharry. As the slope of the shore out into the Beauly Firth
from Clachnaharry is not steep, it was necessary to construct the sea
lock about 1,200ft (367m) out into the Firth, in order that ships could
enter or leave the canal at any state of the tide. In fact the British Waterways Board's general rule is that ships may pass from four hours before

Plate 64 The flight of four locks at Muirtown (*Derrick Beckett*)

Plate 65 Muirtown Basin, with a lock gate lifting-boat moored in readiness (*Derrick Beckett*)

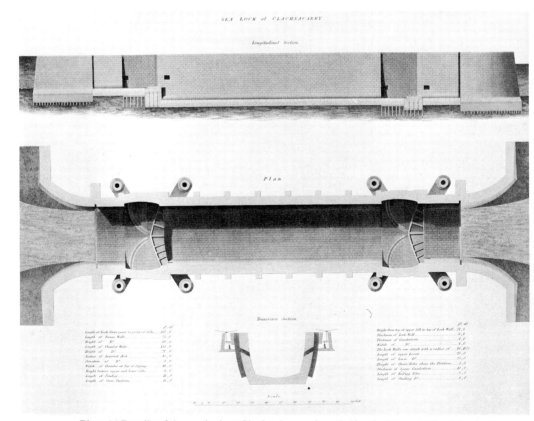

Plate 66 Details of the sea lock at Clachnaharry (*from* Telford's Atlas, *Richard Packer*)

Plate 67 The embankments built next to the sea lock at Clachnaharry with Beauly Firth on the right (*Derrick Beckett*)

to four hours after high water. This also applies at Corpach. Telford and Jessop had originally proposed to construct the sea locks at Clachnaharry and Corpach by building rubble embankments out from the shore. At the site of the locks it was intended to erect cofferdams — wooden enclosures which allow material within them to be excavated and which control ingress of water, generally with the assistance of pumps — and build the stone sea locks inside them. Details of the sea lock at Clachnaharry are shown in Plate 66, which is taken from *Telford's Atlas*. This technique was successful at Corpach, but not at Clachnaharry.

The embankments (Plate 67) were built to the position at which the lock was to be constructed. It was found that there was 55ft (17m) of mud on top of a solid bottom. It was not possible to drive the oak piles which formed part of the cofferdam through the mud and an alternative solution had to be found. The area in which the lock was to be constructed was weighted with rubble from a nearby quarry and built up to a higher level than that of the embankments, then left for six months. This pre-loading consolidated the mud and it was then possible to complete driving of the piles and to construct the cofferdam.

Organisation of the construction, labour and materials

Jessop's role in the construction of the canal was that of a consultant; it was Telford who was responsible for detailed aspects of the construction of the canal and the organisation of the labour force, materials,

Table 5

Clachnaharry, 17 August 1811	Counters and overseers	Masons and quarrymen	Carpenters and sawyers	Blacksmiths and hammermen	Labourers by measure	Labourers by day	Sailors	Total
At Dochfour and Dochgarroch	1	1	5		112	12		131
At Kinmylies			1		38	2		41
At sea lock, etc.	2	38	7	3	129	18		197
At Redcastle	1	15		1	36			53
Employed in carriage of stone							8	8
Totals	4	54	13	4	315	32	8	430

Corpach, 17 August 1811	Counters and overseers	Masons and quarrymen	Carpenters and sawyers	Blacksmiths and hammermen	Labourers by measure	Labourers by day	Sailors	Total
At sea lock and Corpach Basin	1	176	8	4				189
At locks, Corpach Moss					90			90
At Muirshearlich					248			248
At Strone	1		4	2				7
At East and West Moy	1	24			95			120
At regulating lock, etc.		106			123			229
At Fassfern Quarry		26						26
At Lismore Quarry		4						4
At Cumbraes Quarry		30						30
Employed in carriage of stone							12	12
Totals	3	366	12	6	556		12	955
Total persons employed								1385

transport, land purchase and finance. Construction work commenced in December 1803 and from 1804 to 1812 an annual joint inspection of the works was made, with Telford making an additional visit. From 1812 an annual inspection was made by Telford. This frequency of inspection by Jessop and Telford seems hardly adequate for a project of such magnitude, but in 1803 Telford recruited a competent project team, a number of whom had worked for him previously in England and Wales. The work was split into two districts, eastern and western, with resident superintendents based at Clachnaharry and Corpach. These were as follows:

Clachnaharry	*Corpach*
M. Davidson (1804–19)	J. Telford (1804–7)
J. Davidson (1819–22)	A. Easton (1807–22)

John Telford was not a relative of Telford's, but had previously been employed by the Ellesmere Canal Company. However, the level of supervision was not sufficient to control the contractors adequately and much of the masonry work was substandard, in particular at Banavie.

Construction work commenced with the sea locks and basins at Corpach and Clachnaharry, the work then progressing inland. This facilitated the transport of materials to the central section of the canal. The location and transport of materials was a critical factor in the progress of the works. Cast iron was required for a number of purposes: railings, lock gates and the swing bridges (eg Moy bridge). Considerable lengths of railing (horse-drawn waggons) were required at the eastern and western ends of the canal. With the exception of the two sea locks which were constructed of Welsh oak, the lock gates were of cast iron sheathed with Memel pine. Some of the iron for the locks was cast at Jessop's Butterley Ironworks in Derbyshire, transported via the River Trent from Gainsborough to Hull and then by sea to Clachnaharry. The labour force reached a peak in 1811 and Table 5 shows the numbers involved.

By 1818 the eastern and western sections were nearing completion, but the central section between Fort Augustus and the east end of Loch Lochy was not completed until 1822. Although the construction of the canal took about 18 years and the final cost was several times the original estimate, it remains a remarkable civil engineering achievement, providing a 60 mile (97km) shipping route between the North Sea and the Atlantic Ocean. Until recently there was no restriction in headroom for ships using the canal, as swing bridges were provided throughout. Ironically, this has recently changed with the construction of the cable-stayed bridge carrying the A9 over the Moray Firth between Inverness and North Kessock. The headroom for this bridge is 90ft (27.5m).

CALEDONIAN CANAL

Dimensions of the Sea Lock at Clachnaharry
[taken from *Telford's Atlas*]

	Ft.	In.
Length of lock from point to point of sills	180	0
Length of Recess Walls	23	0
Height of Recess Walls	30	6
Length of Chamber Walls	135	0
Height of Chamber Walls	27	6
Radius of Inverted Arch	45	0
Curvature of Inverted Arch	3	0
Width of Chamber at top of Coping	40	0
Height between upper and lower sills	8	0
Length of Forebay	11	0
Length of Stone Platform	16	0
Height from top of upper Sill to top of Lock Wall	21	6
Thickness of Lock Wall	6	0
Thickness of Counterforts	4	0
Width of Counterforts	4	0
The lock walls are struck with a radius of	86.10%	
Length of upper Invert	20	0
Length of lower Invert	25	0
Height of chain holes above the Platform	5	6
Thickness of large Counterforts	10	0
Length of Bearing Piles	5	0
Length of Sheeting Piles	6	0

8
ROADS AND BRIDGES
IN SCOTLAND

The Empire at large being deeply interested in these improvements, as it regards promoting the Fisheries, and increasing the revenue and Population of the Kingdom, justifies government in granting aid towards making Roads and Bridges in a Country which must otherwise remain, perhaps for ages to come, thus imperfectly connected.

(TELFORD, *A survey and report of the coasts and Central Highlands*, 1802)

Thomas Telford's involvement in the construction of the Caledonian Canal between 1803 and 1822 was only part of his massive contribution to the improvement of communications in the Highlands and Lowlands of Scotland. The extract above from Telford's report on his second survey of the coasts and highlands of Scotland demonstrates his views on the importance of improving communications by road in Scotland. In addition to the Commission for the Caledonian Canal (see Chapter 7), the 1803 Act provided for a further Commission for Highland Roads and Bridges, which was also given responsibility for fishing harbours and ports. Both Commissions were served by the same staff. The extent of the civil engineering works extended from Thurso in the north to Carlisle in the south (see Fig 17). Well over 1,000 miles (1,620 km) of roads were constructed in the period 1803 to 1825 and a similar number of bridges. Sir Alexander Gibb's book, *The Story of Telford*, 1935, includes an extensive list of the principal works with which Telford was connected, including roads and bridges. If to this list is added the civil engineering works associated with the Exchequer Bill Loan Commission (see Chapter 1), a detailed description of all these works would occupy several volumes. In this chapter a selection of Telford's road and bridge works in Scotland will be described (see also Gazetteer, p173-6).

Carlisle to Glasgow Road

It is convenient to start from the south and work northwards, although this is not the chronological order of construction. The most important of Telford's works in the Lowlands was the 93 mile (150km) long Carlisle to Glasgow road passing through Elvanfoot and Hamilton. By the be-

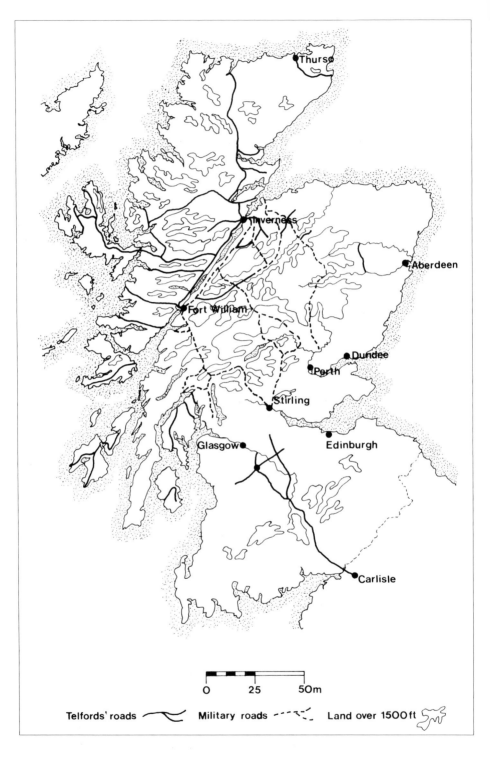

Fig 17 Telford's road network in Scotland

ginning of the nineteenth century, this road had badly deteriorated and was causing serious delays to the London to Glasgow mail coaches which operated on this route from 1788. Following the Act of 1816, £50,000 was granted by Parliament for its reconstruction, 69 miles of which were built under Telford's direction. The remaining 24 miles were under the direction of local trustees.

The line of Telford's road follows the greater part of the A74(T), which also follows the line of a Roman road presumably built prior to the construction of the Antonine Wall across the Clyde–Forth isthmus, circa AD 140. Motorists using the A74(T) can be thankful to Telford for its generally excellent alignment and shallow gradients, about one in thirty being the maximum. The road was designed for durability and Samuel Smiles describes its construction as follows:

The bed was to be formed in two layers, rising about four inches towards the centre — the bottom course being of stones seven inches in depth. These were to be carefully set by hand, with the broadest ends downwards, all cross-banded or jointed, no stone being more than three inches wide on the top. The spaces between them were then to be filled up with smaller stones, packed by hand, so as to bring the whole to an even and firm surface. Over this a top course was to be laid, seven inches in depth, consisting of properly broken hard whinstones, none exceeding six ounces in weight, and each to be able to pass through a circular ring, two inches and a half in diameter [see Fig 1, p12]; a binding of gravel, about half an inch in thickness being placed over all. A drain crossed under the bed of the bottom layer to the outside ditch in every hundred yards.

A less comprehensive specification was adopted for the Highland roads.

Cartland Crags Bridge

Another important Telford road was built across Lanarkshire between 1820 and 1823 to form a link between the cattle areas and Carlisle and the West of Scotland. To construct this road, it was necessary to cross a number of deep ravines and one of the most impressive structures on the route is Cartland Crags Bridge near Lanark. The bridge now carries the A73(T) and it spans the Mouse Water with three stone arches of 62ft (19m). The elevation shown in Plate 68 is taken from *Telford's Atlas*, the height of the soffit of the central arch at the crown being 122ft (37.3m) above water level. This increases to 129ft (39.4m) at the top of the parapet.

Erection of the three stone arches was achieved by constructing timber staging which takes support from the piers and the sides of the ravine. Access to the bottom of the ravine is difficult and the view shown (Plate 69) was taken from a convenient parking area to one side of the

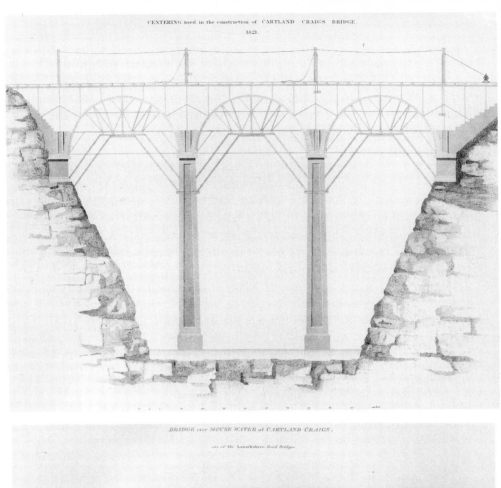

CENTERING used in the construction of CARTLAND CRAIGS BRIDGE.
1821.

BRIDGE over MOUSE WATER at CARTLAND CRAIGS.
one of the Lanarkshire Road Bridges.

Scale of feet

bridge. On the other side of the road from the parking area, there is a toll-house of obvious Telford design. The bridge was completed in 1822 and as with other Telford bridges (see Montford Bridge, Chapter 2) the bridge was widened at a later date by the provision of a cantilevered footway.

Broomielaw Bridge, Glasgow

The name Broomielaw derives from the fact that the banks of the River Clyde in the middle of the eighteenth century were covered with broom (a yellow-flowered shrub). The first Broomielaw bridge was built to the design of William Mylne (younger brother of Robert Mylne) and consisted of seven segmental stone arches erected on poor ground between 1768 and 1772. This structure required extensive repairs during its fifty-year life and was too narrow to accommodate the increasing vehicle traffic crossing the Clyde. A new seven-span segmental arch bridge was designed by Telford and construction commenced in March 1833. It had an overall length of 560ft (171m) and the carriageway, 60ft (18m) wide, was exceptionally wide for that period. The elevation was similar to that adopted by Telford at Bewdley (see Chapter 2) and Dunkeld: an odd number of spans and the arch spans diminishing symmetrically from the central span to the river banks, ranging from 58ft 6in (18m) to 52ft (16m).

It was completed in January 1836 after Telford's death at a cost of £34,427 (T. Ruddock) and demolished in 1899.

Dean Bridge, Edinburgh

Dean Bridge, constructed between 1829 and 1831 at a cost of £18,556 (T. Ruddock) remains as built. It crosses the Waters of Leith and consists of four 90ft (27.5m) span stone arches; the 39ft (12m) wide carriageway is 106ft (32m) above the level of the stream. The bridge has a number of interesting features and is arguably a more successful design than Over Bridge, completed in 1830, and described in Chapter 2. In order to reduce weight the piers and arches are of hollow construction; they are described as follows in Telford's *Life*:

Plate 68 Details of the construction of Cartland Crags Bridge (*from* Telford's Atlas, *Richard Packer*)

Plate 69 Cartland Crags Bridge carries the A73(T) over Mouse Water (*from* Telford's Atlas, *Richard Packer*)

The piers are built internally with hollow compartments, as at the Menai Bridge, the side walls being 3 feet thick and the cross walls 2 feet. Projecting from the piers and abutments are pilasters (pillar built out from a wall) of solid masonry. The main arches have their springing 70 feet from the foundations, and rise 30 feet: and at 20 feet higher, other arches of 96 feet span and 10 feet rise, are constructed: the face of these, projecting before the main arches and spandrels, producing a distinct external soffit of 5 feet in breadth. This with the peculiar piers, constitutes the principal distinctive feature of the bridge.

Above the arch rings, outer and inner spandrels were built up and stone slabs were placed across the voids between the spandrels. Above these stones were placed broken stone, a clay seal and a layer of lime concrete. The original pavement consisted of gravel and broken stone. The current road surface is asphalt with a layer of steel mesh reinforced concrete below. In contrast to Over Bridge and Perronet's Neuilly Bridge over the River Seine, there has been little evidence of any movement of the structure of Dean Bridge in over 150 years.

Dunkeld Bridge

The difficulties of travelling through the Central Highlands of Scotland at the beginning of the nineteenth century were strongly expressed by Lord Henry Cockburn, a member of the Bar travelling on the northern circuit:

Those who are born to modern travelling can scarcely be made to understand how the previous age got on. The state of the roads may be judged from two or three facts. There was no bridge over the Tay at Dunkeld, or over the Spey at Fochabers, or over the Findhorn at Forres. Nothing but wretched pierless ferries, let to poor cottars, who rowed, or hauled, or pushed a crazy boat across, or more commonly got their wives to do it.

Telford in his report on the Highlands observed that the route from Edinburgh to Inverness through the Central Highlands was seriously interrupted at Dunkeld. Dunkeld could be considered as the entrance to the Central Highlands and the bridge formed a connection between existing lines of road which were subsequently improved.

Robert Southey claimed that Dunkeld Bridge, with some justification, was one of the finest in Scotland (Plate 70). It was constructed between 1806 and 1809 and admirably demonstrates Telford's aesthetic perception and technical ability. The seven arch spans are as follows:

feet	20	74	84	90	84	74	20
metres	6.1	22.6	25.7	27.5	25.7	22.6	6.1

Plate 70 Dunkeld Bridge over the River Tay, opened in 1809, admirably demonstrates Telford's aesthetic perception and technical ability *(Derrick Beckett)*

The 20ft land arches are semicircular and the remainder segmental. The proportions are elegant and the appearance of the bridge is improved by adopting an odd number of arch spans, the maximum at the centre and decreasing segmentally towards the river bank. According to Southey, the bridge was constructed on dry ground, formerly the bed of the river. Gravel, brought down from a tributary of the Tay upstream of Dunkeld, diverted the channel of the Tay. On completion of the bridge the original river bed was cleared. This possibly accounts for the low cost of the bridge, about £14,000. It was partly financed by the Duke of Atholl, whose conifer plantations can be seen on the surrounding hills, which rise to a height of 1,200ft (367m).

The abutments and arch spandrels are hollow in order to reduce the self weight of the structure, and it has some non-structural ornamentation: the keystone courses project over the full width of the soffits of the arches and solid semicircular turrets were built between the arch spans (see Plate 70). As a general rule, the appearance of a bridge is not improved by ornamentation, but Dunkeld Bridge is arguably an exception to this rule. It stands today, as built, but with a weight limit of 32 tons (320kN) or an 11 ton (110kN) axle load.

Bonar and Craigellachie Bridges

Telford's bridge at Craigellachie (literal translation 'the neck of separation'), spanning 150ft (46m) over the River Spey and completed in 1815, is one of a number of examples of his mastery in designing and constructing bridges in cast iron. Several of these have been described previously — Holt Fleet, Mythe and Galton. At first sight it seems an irrational decision to adopt ironwork which was cast in Wales and then transported by canal and ship to the North of Scotland. However, in 1811 Telford had made the decision to adopt cast iron for a bridge even further north than Craigellachie — at Bonar, which is at the head of the Dornoch Firth. Bonar Bridge was part of the main route to the north, with major bridges at the following locations:

Dunkeld over the River Tay	stone
Lovat over the River Beauly	stone
Bonar at the head of the Dornoch Firth	cast iron

Telford was well aware of the destructive effects of the flow of water in Highland rivers, which was exacerbated by floating logs and debris. Some local information was sometimes available but there was no reliable hydrological information to hand and Telford's awareness of the problems involved is demonstrated in the following extract from one of his reports to the Commissioners:

In Highland rivers, where in general the stream has not been noticed with any correctness, it is only by degrees that the proper dimensions of bridges can be ascertained: that is in rainy seasons only, and by continuing the observations through a succession of these seasons.

However, in order to meet the construction programme, instant decisions had to be made, which was the probable cause of a number of failures resulting from floods, including that of a bridge over the River Spey at Fochabers.

A span of 100ft (31m) was at the upper limit of stone arches designed by Telford, although there is one exception: Over Bridge spanning the River Severn at Gloucester, of 150ft (46m) span and completed in 1825 (see Chapter 3). As we have seen (Chapter 1), Telford had confidence in the use of cast-iron bridges for spans up to 600ft (183m) and thus to provide a clear span and avoid the introduction of intermediate supports vulnerable to floods, cast iron was adopted at Bonar and Craigellachie.

Some misleading information was provided with regard to the ground conditions. It was originally assumed that both abutments could be founded on rock, but on further investigation poor ground was revealed in the south bank and it was necessary to construct two stone arches of 50ft (15.3m) and 60ft (18.3m) span. The contractors were Simpson & Cargill and the cost of the bridge was just under £14,000. As indicated previously, the ironwork was cast in Wales:

The iron work was cast at the Foundry of Mr. Hazledine at Pontcysyllte in Denbighshire, where for the greater certainty — the arch itself was fitted together on temporary abutments and scaffolding in June last and when found perfect in every particular, was taken to pieces, carried by canal conveyance to Chester, and shipped for the Dornoch Firth where it all arrived safe in the beginning of September; and the centering of the arch being already fixed and fitted for its reception, the iron castings were speedily reconstructed in their proper form, after which the upper part of the masonry, the road-way, and iron railings was finished, and the whole bridge being completed in all its parts, was finally inspected and approved in the beginning of November last — one year early.

(Fourth Report of Commissioners, 1809)

Bonar Bridge was destroyed in 1892, but until then survived the effects of ice, floods, logs and impact from a ship which lost a mast. Robert Southey records 'a remarkable anecdote' concerning the bridge. An inhabitant of Sutherland, whose father was drowned in an accident to a ferry boat crossing the Dornoch Firth in 1809, could not bear to use the ferry again and was thus unable to travel southwards until the bridge was built. On his first use of the bridge he recalled: 'As I went along the road by the side of the water I could see no bridge: at last I came in sight of something like a spiders web in the air — if this be it, thought I, it will never do! But presently, I came upon it, and oh, it is the finest thing that ever was made by God or man!'

Fortunately, Craigellachie has survived the ravages of the River Spey. An elevation and plan taken from *Telford's Atlas* are shown in Plate 71.

It can be seen from Fig 6 (p23) that it was necessary to cut into the rock to form one of the approach roads which turns through ninety degrees at the abutment. An interesting feature of the bridge is the four castellated towers erected at the bridge abutments. There is no technical justification for the ornamentation, and arguably the appearance of the bridge would be improved without them.

The same moulds were used for casting the arch ribs at Bonar and Craigellachie. There are four arch ribs for each bridge which, for ease of transportation, were cast in sections. The rib sections, 3ft (0.92m) deep and 2.5in (64mm) thick, are flanged at their ends and bolted together by cross plates which connect all four ribs transversely. Additional bracing is provided between the arch ribs, and above the ribs vertical X-members form the connection between the arch ribs and the deck. The cross section of the X-members is similar to that adopted for the supports to the Longdon on Tern aqueduct (see Chapter 1). Craigellachie Bridge was completed in 1815 at a cost of £8,000, much less than Bonar, as a result of duplicity of castings and firmer strata. In 1963 it was rebuilt in welded steelwork above the level of the arch ribs.

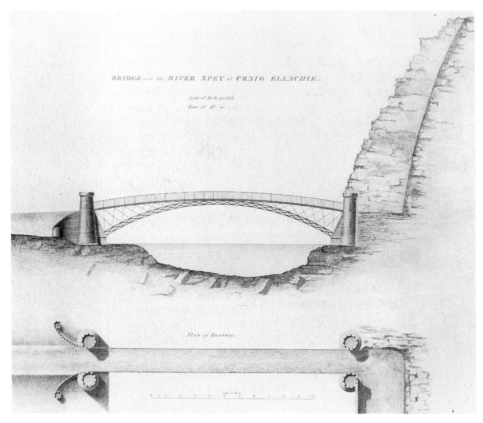

Plate 71 Details of Craigellachie Bridge (*from* Telford's Atlas, *Richard Packer*)

Fassfern and Invermoriston Bridges

The stone bridges at Fassfern and Invermoriston (see Gazetteer, p174-5, for location) are typical of hundreds of minor stone arch bridges required for the Highland road network. Two such roads running westwards, from the line of the Caledonian Canal, are the Fort William to Arisaig road and that from Loch Ness through Glen Moriston to the Kyle of Lochalsh. Fassfern is on the route of the former and has further significance in that rubble stone quarried from this area was transported by boat along Loch Eil to the Caledonian Canal. Plate 72, taken just below the bridge at Fassfern, is indicative of the turbulent nature of Highland streams. The arch and parapets were built of local stone (Plates 72 and 73) and the road is about 12ft (3.7m) at its narrowest point. It was erected c1803 and, as can be seen from the photographs, is still in use.

The two-span arch bridge at Invermoriston, near the start of the road from Loch Ness through Glen Moriston, is a much greater tourist attraction and is referred to as 'The Old Bridge, Invermoriston'. The fol-

Plate 72 Fassfern Bridge is typical of hundreds of minor arch bridges constructed for the Highland road network *(Derrick Beckett)*

Plate 73 The road to the Isles at Fassfern *(Derrick Beckett)*

Plate 74 Lovat Bridge over the River Beauly *(Derrick Beckett)*

lowing description is on a plaque erected by the Leisure and Recreational Department, Highland Regional Council:

The bridge was one of nearly a thousand built by Thomas Telford between 1803 and 1819 as part of a general plan to improve Highland communications. The plan also included the Caledonian Canal built between 1803 and 1823. The absence of bridges was one of the main weaknesses of the Highland road system at that time, and the bridge was an improvement to the existing military road between Inverness and Fort Augustus. It was started in 1805, but delays caused by a 'languid and inattentive contractor' and 'idle workers' resulted in a financial loss of £2,000 for the Guarantor, Sir John Campbell of Archnamurchan, before final completion in 1813. The bridge has suffered considerable vandalism in recent years. Please help conserve it by not disturbing the stonework.

In spite of the vandalism, the stone arches are still intact (Plate 75) and there are fine views of the surrounding hills. The flow of the stream over the rock outcrops and under the arch soffit is spectacular.

Lovat Bridge

As we have seen, Lovat Bridge over the River Beauly is one of the major bridges on the route to the North and was constructed between 1811 and 1814. The five spans are as follows:

feet	40	50	60	50	40
metres	12.2	15.3	18.3	15.3	12.2

The proportioning of the arch spans, gradually increasing towards the centre of the bridge, is similar to Dunkeld Bridge but on a smaller scale. In contrast to Dunkeld Bridge there is no ornamentation and the parapet has a much greater curvature in elevation (Plate 74). Following the collapse of one pier during severe flooding in 1894, two of the red sandstone arches were rebuilt. As with Montford Bridge, which still carries the A5(T) over the River Severn, Lovat Bridge carried the A9(T) over the River Beauly until it was bypassed. In 1982 the route of the A9(T) was diverted via Kessock Bridge over the Beauly Firth, but Lovat Bridge still forms an important link in the regional road network. The Highland Regional Council had been aware for some time that there was significant cracking and spalling in the original three arch spans (J. Danby). Sandstone is known to be vulnerable to deterioration by frost action and inspections revealed that cracking and spalling of the sandstone was largely confined to the north side of the bridge. The repair works were carried out in 1985 over a period of 10 weeks. This included waterproofing the whole of the bridge deck.

Lovat Bridge is a category B listed building and a scheduled ancient monument and thus it was necessary to seek the approval of the Historic

Plate 75 The arches of the 'Old Bridge, Invermoriston' have survived extensive vandalism (*Derrick Beckett*)

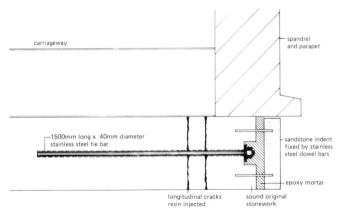

Fig 18 Typical repairs to the cracking and spalling in the sandstone voussoirs of Lovat Bridge

Buildings and Monuments branch of the Scottish Development Department prior to carrying out the works. The Department required that repairs to exposed stonework should be carried out in a matching sandstone. There was no local stone available and the sandstone had to be transported over two hundred miles from Gorse Hill quarry in Dumfriesshire (now Dumfries and Galloway), the county of Telford's birthplace.

It appears that the cracks ran longitudinally in the direction of span of the arches about 300 to 600mm from the external faces of the voussoirs. Spalling was concentrated at the crown and springings of the arches and it was necessary to fix new sandstone facings to 35 of the voussoirs. The voussoirs are typically 500mm deep and extend up to 1,200mm across the width of the arches. Fig 18 illustrates how the new sandstone facings were fixed by means of stainless steel dowel bars and epoxy resin mortar to the original stone. The longitudinal cracks were sealed by resin injection and tie bars were employed to fix the arch edges back to sound material. The total cost of the repair works was in the order of £150,000 and is a good example of modern repair technology being used to extend the useful life of an ageing bridge. The cost of complete replacement of the bridge would be several million pounds.

Kirk Laggan Bridge

Designs by Palladio for wooden bridges have been referred to in the Introduction and although wood has been used extensively for bridge construction, relatively few early examples remain. The use of wood for bridge construction has been hampered by durability problems, difficulties in obtaining sections of adequate cross section and length, and technical problems with connections. Ruddock refers to the pro-

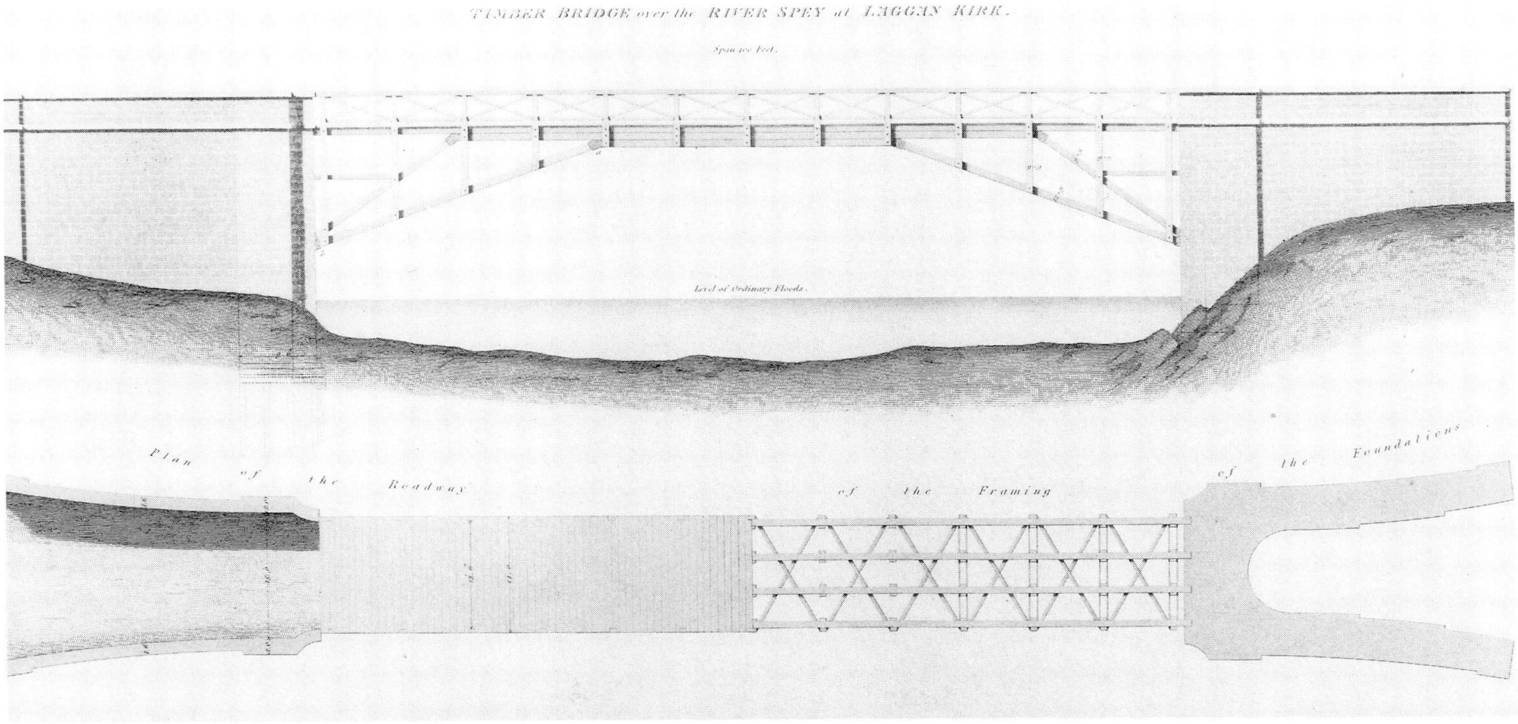

TIMBER BRIDGE over the RIVER SPEY at LAGGAN KIRK.

Span 150 Feet.

level at Ordinary Floods.

Plan of the Roadway of the Framing of the Foundations

Plate 76 Kirk Laggan Bridge, an example of Telford's limited use of wood for bridge construction (*from* Telford's Atlas, *Richard Packer*)

ceedings in the Act for building a bridge at Westminster (1757): '. . . many persons of judgement and taste were extremely disgusted at the thought of a wooden bridge'.

Even today, some engineers are reluctant (arguably unjustifiably) to consider the use of timber for bridge construction in spite of improvements in assessing strength properties, connection design and preservation techniques. It was left to Isambard Kingdom Brunel to really exploit the potential of wood for bridge construction (see *Brunel's Britain*). Telford used wood to a limited extent for bridge construction, but generally as a replacement for bridges which had been destroyed. An example of this is Kirk Laggan Bridge over the River Tay (Plate 76). It was completed in 1828 (now replaced) and cost £1,400, according to a report of the repair commissioners in 1829.

In order to reduce the effective span of the deck, raking struts were introduced which carried the load back to the abutments. Thus the deck was reduced to five relatively short spans, the maximum being in the centre of the bridge between the inner struts. In the central region three deck beams were required: an early example of lamination. This technique together with raking struts was subsequently adopted by Brunel.

The extent of Telford's work on road construction in the Highlands required delegation of supervision coupled with occasional inspections, such as that with Robert Southey and John Rickman in 1819. Six divisions were set up, each with its own superintendent. Telford's deputy in Scotland between 1809 and 1824 was John Mitchell. Mitchell rose from the position of working mason to general superintendent of Highland roads with overall responsibility, under Telford, for the six divisions. His work involved travelling several thousand miles a year and his contribution to the overall programme of construction was invaluable.

THOMAS TELFORD AND THE DEVELOPMENT OF MECHANISED TRANSPORT

. . . Is Inland Navigation to be ruined by these Railroad Projectors. If so Canal Proprietors had better stop all further improvement and then what will soon be the state of the country . . .

The above is an extract from a letter written by the chairman of the Trent and Mersey Canal Committee to Thomas Telford in the summer of 1824.

By 1824 the activities of the 'rail-roaders' were such that it was not possible for canal companies, turnpike trusts and coach operators to ignore the threat of a new transportation system: the steam locomotive and track pioneered by George and Robert Stephenson. In 1822, T. Gray in *Observations on a General Iron Way* proposed a plan of a general iron way for Great Britain (see *Stephensons' Britain*). London was the focal point with lines radiating to about twenty major towns and cities.

It is not generally appreciated that Telford had a significant involvement in the development of railways. In order to put this in perspective it is necessary to trace the early development of railways.

Wagons with wooden flanged wheels running along wooden tracks were in use in the sixteenth century. Subsequently, strips of iron were fixed to the top of wooden rails and various shapes of iron were designed to replace wooden rails. At the end of the eighteenth century, there were two types of railway in use: the edge rail of T or I section, which was used in conjunction with a flanged iron wheel, and the L-section plate rail with a vertical flange on the rail, not on the wheel. The distance between the rails was governed by the width required for a horse to walk within them – about 4ft (1.2m).

As we have seen, Telford worked extensively with William Jessop (see Chapters 3 and 7), and Jessop was engineer to the Surrey Iron Railway which was opened in July 1803. It was the first public goods railway to be sanctioned by Parliament and ran between Wandsworth and Croydon. The track consisted of 3ft (0.92m) span L-section plate rails spanning between stone blocks. The wagons had a gross weight of 3 tons (30kN) and were normally drawn in a chain of five by a single horse (C. Hadfield and A. W. Skempton). However, by 1803, Richard Trevithick (1771–1833) had successfully built two steam-powered road locomotives (steam carriages) and a year later built a steam locomotive to run on L-section plate rails a distance of 9¾ miles (15.7km) from Penydarren ironworks to the Glamorganshire Canal.

In 1808 Trevithick made a final attempt to demonstrate the potential of the steam locomotive and an engine, *Catch me who can*, was built to run on a circular track near Euston Square. It was not a commercial success and it was left to others to develop the steam locomotive to a stage at which it could seriously challenge the horse.

The period 1810 to 1825 was one of continuous progress in locomotive and track development, with contributions by John Blenkinsop, Matthew Murray, William Hedley and George and Robert Stephenson. George Stephenson began working on the design of steam locomotives in 1813 and by about 1820 had carried out an extensive series of trials in relation to both track and locomotive design. On the Hetton and Killingworth colliery lines the locomotives ran at about 4mph (6k/h), pulling a load of 64 tons (640kN).

The work was of great interest to the promoters of the Liverpool & Manchester Railway and an independent report was prepared for them by Charles Sylvester, a civil engineer. He concluded that locomotives in their current state of development were a great improvement on the employment of horse power and that they were capable of 'so much improvement'.

Telford's involvement with the Liverpool & Manchester Railway, which was formally opened in September 1830, will be discussed later, but it is also necessary to refer to the opening of the Stockton & Darlington Railway in 1825, a year prior to the completion of Telford's Menai Suspension Bridge. The first Act for the Stockton & Darlington Railway was given royal assent in April 1821 and ten months later George Stephenson was appointed engineer at a salary of £660 per annum. The first passenger service commenced in October 1825 with a daily horse-drawn coach. It was not until 1834 that the locomotive replaced the horse for both passenger and goods trains.

Thus it can be seen that in mid-1824 when Telford received the letter from the chairman of the Trent and Mersey Canal Committee, the locomotive had by no means been generally accepted as a viable means of transportation. This did not apply to the Stephensons, who were sufficiently optimistic about its potential to open a locomotive works in June 1823. Telford was in an awkward position. Obviously he could not ignore railway development but his long-term association with canals and the relationships and loyalties developed could not be dismissed overnight. Telford acted by sending an assistant to inspect the Stockton & Darlington Railway and subsequently observed that all traffic would have to be handled by the company which owned the line (A. Dalgleish). Other than the payment of tolls, canals and roads were available for use by anyone (A. Dalgleish) and canal companies were not permitted to trade on their own. Freedom of use could not apply to railways and this was a perceptive observation by Telford.

Telford's involvement in the Liverpool & Manchester Railway resulted from his appointment as technical adviser to the Exchequer Bill Loan Commission (see Chapter 1). The promoters applied to the commission for financial assistance and Telford was called in to prepare a report. The Liverpool & Manchester Railway had an unhappy early history. George Stephenson was appointed engineer in the summer of 1824 and the petition for a Bill was presented to the House of Commons in February 1825. In the witness box Stephenson was brutally exploited by the opposing counsel: 'This is the most absurd scheme that ever entered into the head of a man to conceive'. The cross-examination revealed surveying errors and guessed estimates, and the Bill was thrown out. Stephenson was relieved of his post and following further work by the Rennies and Vignoles, the Bill received royal assent in May 1826. In June 1826 Stephenson was reappointed as principal engineer with Vignoles as his assistant. It was an unhappy relationship: Vignoles resigned six months later and Stephenson was left free to build the line his own way.

It was not until January 1829 that Telford inspected the works and was accompanied by Stephenson. Telford, with his immense experience of organising major civil engineering projects, must have been somewhat concerned about the general lack of organisation, but his report was not too critical. However, it satisfied the railway company, which resulted in Telford issuing a second and more critical report. The year 1829 was a testing one in Stephenson's career as the method of traction had not been resolved. Telford condemned the use of cable haulage with the motive power being provided by stationary engines, which was still being considered. He recommended the use of horses or locomotives and in order to obtain a loan of £100,000, a company was formed to act quickly. This led to the 'Grand Competition of Locomotives on the Liverpool and Manchester Railway' and trials were commenced in October 1829. The Stephensons entered the *Rocket*, built at their Newcastle works. Briefly, the *Rocket* was the only locomotive to fulfil all the conditions and it achieved an average speed of 24mph (33.6k/h) with a load of 12.75 tons (127kN) — three times its weight. The *Rocket* could

also negotiate an incline of 1 in 96 at Whiston (see *Stephensons' Britain*).
Thus with the official opening of the line in September 1830, the
Stephensons had established the validity of a means of traction that did
not become obsolete until the demise of the steam engine some 130
years later.

By the time of Telford's death in 1834, work was in progress on the 80
mile (129km) Grand Junction Railway between Warrington and Birmingham (George Stephenson and Joseph Locke) and the 112 mile
(180km) London & Birmingham Railway (Robert Stephenson), and the
28 year old Isambard Kingdom Brunel had been appointed engineer to
the proposed 118 mile (190km) Great Western Railway between London and Bristol. By 1860 the route mileage exceeded 7,500 miles
(12,070km).

The impact of railways on roads and canals was immediate and
severe: within two and a half years of the opening of the Liverpool &
Manchester Railway the number of coaches plying between the two
cities was reduced from twenty-nine to one. Soon after steam locomotives were able to haul loads several times that by a horse-drawn canal
barge.

However, it is of interest to speculate on whether development of the
railway network would have taken place at such a rapid pace if the same
effort had been applied to the application of steam power to road transport. As early as 1769, a Frenchman, Nicholas Cugnot, built a three-
wheeled steam-powered road vehicle which he drove through the
streets of Paris (R. Syme). The authorities declared it to be dangerous
and Cugnot was imprisoned for his efforts. Fifteen years later William
Murdoch, one of James Watt's assistants, constructed a toy steam engine which was reported to have outrun the speed of its inventor (S.
Smiles). As we have seen, Richard Trevithick continued the development of road locomotives and drove one from Cornwall to London. The
future for road locomotives seemed much brighter when an engineer,
Goldsworthy Gurney, designed a steam coach which in 1827 ran between
Bath and London at an average speed of 9mph (14.5k/h). However,
excessive toll charges made it difficult for steam carriages to operate
economically and in 1831 a Parliamentary Select Committee was set
up to assess the prospects of steam road carriages and toll rates. The
committee reported in favour of reducing tolls and was enthusiastic
about future prospects for steam carriages. Their report concluded that
steam carriages were safe, could negotiate inclines, caused less wear on
road surfaces than horses and most important were cheaper and faster
than horse-drawn carriages. Extensive vested interest resulted in Parliament taking no action, although Telford himself supported the commit-

tee findings. In 1833, Telford became actively involved in promoting the Steam Company to run a service between London and Birmingham, which in due course was to be extended to Holyhead. It had to be demonstrated that a reliable service could be operated and Telford joined John Rickman and others for a trial run in a steam carriage operated by Sir Charles Dance. The trial was not a success: a boiler tube failed and an effective repair was not made. The carriage reached Stony Stratford, 54 miles (87km) from London on the first day and was then abandoned. It was at this time, winter 1833, that Robert Stephenson was staking out the line of the London & Birmingham Railway and frequently stayed at an inn in Stony Stratford. It is unlikely that he was too disappointed to hear that the steam road carriage covered less than half of the journey from London to Birmingham.

It was obviously too late for Telford to further the cause of steam road carriages. Punitive tolls put a stop to significant development but there was a brief revival in the early 1860s. However, in 1865 the 'Red Flag Act' was passed, which reduced the speed of steam cars to 4mph (6.4k/h) in the country and 2mph (3.2k/h) in towns. A minimum crew of three was required, one of whom walked 180ft (55m) in front of the vehicle carrying a red flag. This was the final blow to the development of the steam carriage and the railways forged ahead, reaching a route mileage of 20,000 (32,000km) by 1914.

The situation has now reversed, the railways struggling for survival with a route mileage of about one half of that in 1914. Option A in the 1983 Serpell Report on railway finances contains a mere 1,630 route miles (2,623km). Perhaps Telford was right in favouring roads and if the steam road carriage had been successfully developed earlier in his life, we would not have been left with the Stephensons' legacy. But to many, including the author, this legacy at its best is still the most civilised method of travel.

It would be wrong to state that Telford had no involvement in railways prior to the Liverpool & Manchester: he used them in the construction of the Caledonian Canal and in 1810 surveyed a route for a line between Glasgow and Berwick. Apparently the route was unfavourable for canal construction. He advised on the construction of a horse-drawn goods line between Stratford and Moreton-in-the-Marsh (1821–6) and was named as the engineer for the proposed London to Dover Railway (1824) and the Clarence Railway (1828–9) in the Durham coalfield. The latter two did not come to fruition but it is of interest to note that steam locomotives were proposed. Finally, in 1829 Telford was consulted on the Newcastle & Carlisle Railway. This line was eventually opened in 1839 and the tractive power was locomotive engines! (A. Gibb).

GAZETTEER

As we have seen, Telford's works extended from London to North Wales and the North of Scotland. A gazetteer covering all places of interest associated with the life of Thomas Telford would occupy more than one volume and several weeks of travelling. Most visitors will have a limited amount of time available and thus the contents of this gazetteer are designed to cover the majority of Telford's principal works in about fourteen days. It is suggested that the tour can be split into three independent sections:

1. London: 1 day (London Transport)
2. England and Wales: 5 days (car, 800 miles or 1,300km)
3. Lowlands and Highlands of Scotland: 7–8 days (car, 1,500 miles or 2,400km)

The mileages given for Sections 2 and 3 are for a return trip from London. An alternative for the Scottish tour is to use the Rail Drive/Europcar service (Tel: 01-950 5050) using Carlisle as a starting point. British Rail also operate an overnight Motorail service to Scotland (Tel: 01-387 8541). For hotel accommodation, the following should be contacted:
Welsh Tourist Board, London Office, 34 Piccadilly, London, W1V 9PB (Tel: 01-409 0969);
Scottish Tourist Board, London Office, 19 Cockspur Street, SW1Y 5BL (Tel: 01-930 8661).

There are numerous tourist information centres in Wales and Scotland and the addresses may be obtained from the above.

British Rail's current network, infrequent services in rural areas and Sunday closing of stations, make it impractical to avoid using a car. The tour time would have to be at least doubled and extensive use made of local bus services, if available.

Time spent on planning the route is well worthwhile and the Ordnance Survey Routeplanner of Great Britain, scale 1 : 625,000 (about 1in to 10 miles or 4cm to 25km) is most useful. The Ordnance Survey Atlas of Great Britain, scale 1 : 250,000 (about 1½in to 5 miles or 4cm to 10km) facilitates more detailed planning and for certain locations, eg Telford's birthplace, the Landranger series is more appropriate, scale 1 : 50,000 (1¼in to 1 mile or 2cm to 1km). An illustrated brochure is available free on request from Information and Enquiries, Ordnance Survey, Ramsey Road, Maybush, Southampton SO9 4DH.

The tours indicated previously can be extended to take in other places of interest, for example, the Iron Gorge Museum, Salop, Conwy Castle and Ben Nevis. The preferred time of the year to visit Scotland or Wales is September/October. There are fewer tourists, the roads are less congested and the autumn leaves turning from green to brown provide a magnificent backcloth to many of Telford's works. An umbrella and wellington boots are recommended.

Tour 1: London (Somerset House & St Katharine Docks)

For those not familiar with central London, reference should be made to the *A–Z London Street Atlas* (Geographers' A–Z Map Co Ltd, Tel: 01-242 9246). Take the District or Circle line to Embankment or Temple and walk along the Embankment to Waterloo Bridge. Use the steps to reach the top of the bridge and Somerset House is on the northeast side of the bridge, between the Embankment and the Strand. Between 1782 and 1784 Telford was employed by the architect Sir William Chambers to work as a mason on the corner nearest the bridge (see Plate 4, p36). While in London, Telford was also introduced to another distinguished architect, Robert Adam, who designed a number of notable buildings in London, including the Adelphi Buildings in the Strand, a short distance from Somerset House.

To reach St Katharine Docks, take the District or Circle line from Temple to Tower Hill. Follow the signs to St Katharine Docks. The pedestrian route is via a subway under Tower Hill, skirting the perimeter of the Tower of London and through another subway under Tower Bridge Approach into St Katharine's Way. Walk along St Katharine's Way, which runs parallel to International House, and then turn left with the Tower Hotel on the left, on to the river front. The walls of the entrance lock chamber are original, but the mitred wooden gates and the sills have been reconstructed. The new single steel gates point horizontally and are lowered by cables into the bottom of the lock. The cast-iron swing bridge has gone, but there is an interesting timber pedestrian lift bridge at the river end of the lock. Notice the cast-iron bollards (Plate 77) embossed with the words 'St Katharine Docks 1828'. The dockmaster's house adjacent to the east side of the entrance lock has a similarity in style to the toll-houses on the London to Holyhead road.

Plate 77 A cast-iron bollard embossed 'St Katharine Docks 1828' (*Derrick Beckett*)

Plate 78 The retractable cast-iron footbridge at the entrance to the eastern dock (*Derrick Beckett*)

The Dickens public house, a former brewery, stands on the site of the export shed and Wood Wharf (see Plate 54, p110). The brewery was found about 600ft (180m) away encased in the bricks of a warehouse. The oak framework was picked up and moved bodily to its present site. The entrance to the eastern dock is crossed by an interesting cast-iron footbridge (Plate 78), possibly a Telford design. It consists of two cantilever trusses which can be retracted into the quays by means of a rack mechanism. This design can be contrasted with the recent laminated timber lift bridge which crosses the entrance to the western docks. Adjacent to the timber bridge stands a Coronarium which was unveiled during the Silver Jubilee celebrations of 1977 and stands on the site of the original Church of the Royal Foundation of St Katharine. The cast-iron columns are from the former warehouse A.

The boats are a great attraction and there are a number of historic ships: the *Discovery* is moored in the eastern dock together with the *Nore* lightship. The full extent of Telford's work can only be revealed by emptying the docks. The 33ft (10m) high quay walls have retained water for over 150 years and are an outstanding example of nineteenth century dock works.

Tour 2: England and Wales

If carefully planned, this five-day tour can embrace the London and Holyhead road, Longdon on Tern, Chirk and Pont Cysyllte aqueducts, the bridges over the River Severn and the Menai and Conwy suspension bridges. Starting early from London, Llangollen (180 miles, 288km) can be reached in the first day and is a convenient base for the rest of the tour. There is a wide choice of hotels in the Llangollen area, see Wales Tourist Board publication, *Where to Stay, Hotels and Guest Houses.*

In deference to Thomas Telford, proceed along the A5(T) via Dunstable and Bletchley to Churchover near Rugby. The A5 follows the route of the Roman road Watling Street. At Churchover, turn left on to the A426 and join the M6 at junction 1. (Time can be saved, by using the M1 and joining the M6 at junction 19.)

Location No. 1: Galton Bridge, Smethwick
Proceed along the M6 to Great Barr (junction 7) and turn on to the M5. At junction 1, leave the M5 and follow the A452 (Telford Way) to the junction with the A457. Just prior to the junction, Galton Bridge can be seen on the right-hand side of the road. The bridge carries Roebuck Lane, which is now closed to vehicular traffic. There is access to the bridge from the embankment which leads down to the canal. Impressive views of Telford's cutting can be obtained from the bridge.

Location No 2: Stretton Aqueduct, A5(T) — Watling Street
From Galton Bridge, rejoin the M5 (northbound) at junction 1. Continue on to the M6 (junction 8) and proceed to junction12. Turn left on to the A5(T); a few miles west it is crossed by Stretton Aqueduct, which carries what is now called the Shropshire Union Canal. Note the inscription on the face of the aqueduct: 'Thomas Telford F.R.S. L&E (Fellow of the Royal Society, London and Edinburgh) Engineer 1832, Birmingham and Liverpool Canal'. It is possible to climb the embankment on the left-hand side of the A5(T) and obtain excellent views of the canal, extensively used by pleasure craft.

Location No 3: Longdon on Tern Aqueduct
Continue west along the A5(T) with the Belvide Reservoir on the left, noting the excellent alignment of the road. At the outskirts of Telford New Town, follow the A442 signposted to Whitchurch. At the end of the perimeter road, continue to follow the signposts to Whitchurch and at Crudgington turn left on to the B5062. Travel about 2 miles (3.6km) west and then turn left again, following the B5063 southwards to

Longdon on Tern. A convenient stopping place is the Tayleur Arms. About 300 yards (275m) further south, the B5063 crosses the River Tern via a hump-backed masonry bridge and the aqueduct is in a field to the left of the bridge. Access to the field is at a gate some 50 yards (46m) beyond the bridge. It is necessary to negotiate a barbed wire fence to reach the aqueduct. The canal either side of the aqueduct has long since disappeared and the structure stands in splendid isolation. The construction details are described in Chapter 1.

The time required to inspect Galton Bridge and the two aqueducts, including travelling from London, is about 7 hours and it is recommended that inspection of further locations is left until the following day. Proceed south along the B5063 to the outskirts of Telford New Town and at the first roundabout turn right on to the B4394. Rejoin the A5(T) at Norton. Follow the A5(T) via Shrewsbury and Chirk to Llangollen, about 40 miles (65km). There are numerous hotels in and around Llangollen, but the Chainbridge Hotel (Tel: 0978 860215) is ideally situated in a spectacular setting, sandwiched between the River Dee and the upper reaches of the Llangollen (Ellesmere) Canal near Horseshoe Falls (see Chapter 3). A complete day is recommended for inspection of the following locations in the vicinity of Llangollen.

Location No 4: Horseshoe Falls, Llantysilio
On the western outskirts of Llangollen, the Chain Bridge and Hotel are reached by leaving the A5(T) and turning right and crossing the River Dee (signposted to A542). The canal passes the rear of the hotel. Walk along the canal, passing under bridges 48 and 49 to the gauging house which controls the flow of water, about 8 million gallons a day. Horseshoe Falls are just beyond the gauging house (Plate 79). It is a leisurely hour's walk along the canal to the centre of Llangollen, with a superb view over the town and River Dee. There is a fascinating exhibition of canal history at the Canal Exhibition and Passenger Boat Centre (Tel: Llangollen 860702 for opening times). For further information on places of interest associated with the Llangollen Canal, refer to the Waterways World Guide, *Llangollen Canal* (Waterways World, Kottingham House, Dale Street, Burton upon Trent, Staffordshire DE14 3TD).

Location No 5: Pont Cysyllte Aqueduct
It is about one hour's walk along the canal to the Pont Cysyllte Aqueduct, or alternatively take the A539 towards Ruabon as far as a three-span masonry arch which crosses the River Dee. Parking downstream from the bridge, the highest section of the aqueduct can be

Plate 79 Horseshoe Falls at the summit of the Llangollen (Ellesmere) Canal *(Derrick Beckett)*

seen crossing the River Dee between the steep wooded banks. It is worth walking from the bridge up to Fron Cysyllte; the A5(T) is rejoined near the Aqueduct public house. To the left, a large section of the aqueduct can be seen, giving a good impression of its overall length. The south end of the aqueduct can be approached by walking along a tree-lined embankment. Note the timber lift bridge (bridge 28). Access to the towpath on the east side of the aqueduct requires walking under the arch ribs which span from the abutment to the first pier. To walk along the towpath crossing the River Dee at a height of about 130ft (40m) is a unique experience, but not recommended for those nervous of heights. There is a plaque commemorating the aqueduct's construction which is to be found on the first river pier on the south side:

> Built by Thomas Telford 1795–1805
> There are 18 piers made of local stone,
> The central ones over the Dee being
> 126′ high up to the ironwork.
> The canal runs through an iron trough,
> 1007′ long, 11′ 10″ wide and 5′ 3″ deep,
> The largest in Britain. The iron was
> supplied by William Hazledine from
> his foundaries at Shrewsbury and
> nearby Cefn Mawr.
> Total cost £47,000
> Water is fed from the Dee at the Horseshoe
> Falls at Llantysilio near Llangollen.

The Monsanto chemical works at Cefn Mawr can be seen from the aqueduct towpath and are on the site of William Hazledine's foundry, which was demolished in 1946.

Location No 6: Chirk Aqueduct
Join the A5(T) at the Aqueduct public house travelling back towards Shrewsbury. Chirk is about 4 miles (6.4km) from Pont Cysyllte. On entering the town, turn right on to the B4500 and the road crosses the canal at the entrance to Chirk tunnel. Look down from the road level at the tunnel entrance and the canal can be seen narrowing down to a thin grey line as it crosses the Ceiriog valley via the masonry arches with a cast-iron lining. The railway viaduct is on the right and the river forms the boundary between England and Wales.

Location No 7: Frankton Junction, Montgomeryshire Canal
If time permits, it is well worth the effort to visit the junction of the Ellesmere and Montgomery canals at Frankton Junction. Proceed south from Chirk along the A5(T) and at Whittington turn left and follow the A495 for about 2 miles (3.6km). The canal is crossed at Maestermyn Bridge (No. 5). Frankton Junction is about a mile (1.6km) walk along the towpath, passing under or over bridges 4, 3, 2 and 1 — the

Plate 80 The staircase locks on the Montgomeryshire Canal at Frankton Junction (*Derrick Beckett*)

plaque on bridge 1 states 70. The bridges are numbered from 1 at Hurleston, at the junction with the Shropshire Union Canal, up to 69 prior to reaching Frankton Junction. Beyond Frankton Junction they begin again at 1 (70). It is worth walking a short distance along the Montgomeryshire Canal to the staircase locks (Frankton Locks) (Plate 80).

The third day of the tour involves a 160 mile (256km) return journey from Llangollen to Holyhead and a 15 mile (24km) diversion from Bangor to Conwy, and thus an early start is recommended.

Location No 8: Waterloo Bridge, Betws-y-Coed
From Llangollen proceed along the A5(T) via Corwen. Just after the junction between the A5 and the A470(T), the A5 crosses the River Conwy via Waterloo Bridge. It is possible to park a short distance beyond the bridge. Walk across the field to the river for a distant view of the bridge. It is possible to walk towards the bridge using the rock outcrops (wellington boots essential). For a close-up of the decorative spandrels — rose, leek, shamrock and thistle — walk back across the bridge and bear right. Note also the names 'W. Hazledine, Founder and W. Stuttle, Foreman'.

Location No 9: Nant Ffrancon Pass
Continue through Betws-y-Coed following the A5(T) via Capel Curig and the most spectacular section of the London and Holyhead road is reached. It is here that the alignment and shallow gradient of Telford's road can be fully appreciated. Proceed past Lake Ogwen. The road crosses a small stream with a youth hostel on the left and a short distance further on it is possible to park in a lay-by. Climb 100ft (30m) or so to observe the alignment of the road; a remarkable demonstration of Thomas Tredgold's (1788–1829) classic definition of the scope of civil engineering:

That species of knowledge which constitutes the profession of a Civil Engineer; being the art of directing the great sources of powers in Nature for the use and convenience of man, as the means of production and of traffic in States both for external and internal trade, as applied in the construction of roads, bridges, aqueducts, canals, river navigation and docks, for internal intercourse and exchange; and in the construction of ports, harbours, moles, breakwaters and lighthouses, and in the art of navigation by artificial power for the purposes of commerce; and in the construction and adoption of machinery; and in the drainage of cities and towns.

It is a fitting tribute to Telford's contribution to the art of civil engineering that he was invited to become the first president of the Institution of Civil Engineers.

Location No 10: Menai Bridge

Follow the A5(T) along the Nant Ffrancon Pass and the road gradually descends to the junction with the A55(T). Proceed into Bangor and then follow the signs to the Menai Bridge. It is possible to park at the approaches to the bridge. To obtain the best overall views of the bridge, cross via the footpath on the east side and walk down to the Anglesey shore of the Menai Strait. There is an outcrop of land from which the scale of the structure can be fully appreciated. Note the proportioning of the piers to the approach viaduct. For an overall impression of the bridge and its environment, cross the bridge, turn right and proceed along the A5 towards Llanfairpwllgwyngyll. The bridge can be seen to the left, and from this distance the heaviness of the stiffening girders is lost and its appearance is almost identical to Telford's original design. Pass the approaches and turn left at the Carneg Bren Country Hotel into Church Lane, where it is possible to park close to St Mary's Church. There is a fine view of the Britannia Bridge (now road and rail) which was opened in 1850 to form part of the rail link between Chester and Holyhead (see *Stephensons' Britain*). Until 1970, the deck of Robert Stephenson's Britannia Bridge consisted of two massive wrought-iron tubes about 30ft (9m) deep through which the trains passed. In 1970, a fire caused irreparable damage to the tubes and the deck structure was rebuilt in arch form and the opportunity was taken to provide a combined road and rail link. The piers remain as built.

It is of interest to contrast the appearance of Stephenson's and Telford's bridges and a superb view of Telford's bridge can be obtained by walking up to the road deck of the reconstructed Britannia Bridge. The elegant suspension bridge expresses the timeless beauty of the art of engineering.

Location No 11: Anglesey

Compared with the Nant Ffrancon Pass and the Menai Bridge, Anglesey is an anticlimax; flat, uninteresting and drab villages giving an impression of general decay. However, there are two interesting toll-houses. The first is at Llanfair (abbreviation). At the junction with the road to Brynsiencyn there is a two-storey toll-house (Plate 81), which is of particular interest as it still has its toll boards in place.

The journey across Anglesey is a tedious 20 miles (36km), but at the approaches to Holyhead, the A5(T) crosses Stanley Sands by means of a 4,000ft (1,225m) long embankment. It was opened in 1823 and is 16ft (5m) high and 114ft (35m) wide at the base. At the Holyhead end of the embankment another two-storey toll-house can be seen on the right.

Plate 81 The two-storey toll-house at Llanfair (*Derrick Beckett*)

Location No 12: Conwy Suspension Bridge
Return to the Menai Bridge and into Bangor and follow the A55(T) towards Conwy via Penmaenmawr. The road follows closely the route adopted by Telford and Robert Stephenson's Chester to Holyhead Railway (c1848), which runs below it hugging the coast (Plate 82). On approaching Penmaenbach headland, the A55(T) passes through a tunnel and at the tunnel portal it is possible to park on a section of Telford's old road, which runs round the headland. It is possible to walk along this section of the old road to the east portal of the tunnel.

Proceed to Conwy, passing through the town wall and continue into the centre — and it is best to park when the opportunity arises. It is a short walk from the centre of the town to Conwy Castle. It is well worth the entrance fee to view the suspension bridge from the castle walls (Plate 83). Telford's bridge (1826) is sandwiched between Robert Stephenson's tubular bridge (1848) on the right and the new road bridge on the left, opened in 1959. The A55(T) is now being reconstructed between St Asaph and Aber via Colwyn Bay, thus there will be a fourth crossing of the Conwy estuary via a tunnel. For a change, return to Llangollen via the B5106 or the A470(T) along the Vale of Conwy. Both roads link up with the A5(T) at Betws-y-Coed. Day four covers further locations on the A5(T) between Llangollen and Shrewsbury and the Severn bridges. An early start is recommended.

Plate 82 Penmaenmawr Viaduct and Tunnel with Telford's Holyhead road above (*Science Museum, London*); (*below*) Plate 83 Looking down from the walls of Conwy Castle onto Telford's suspension bridge (*Derrick Beckett*)

Location No 13: Montford Bridge
Proceed from Llangollen along the A5(T) towards Shrewsbury for about 24 miles (38km) and the A5(T) crosses the River Severn at Montford Bridge. It is possible to park at the adjacent public house and walk across the meadow to the river bank. The red sandstone arches quarried from Nescliffe are still in excellent condition almost two hundred years after their erection in 1792. Note the date of the bridge inscribed on the parapet and the toll-house nearby.

Location No 14: Holyhead Road milepost
Continue along the A5(T) from Montford towards Shrewsbury and the milepost (HOLYHEAD 104–M, SALOP 2M–6F) can be seen on the right-hand side of the road (Plate 84), close to the bypass.

Time permitting, a diversion into Shrewsbury can be made to inspect the castle and gaol on which Telford worked from 1786 (see Chapter 1). Alternatively, proceed round the bypass A5(T) and the road crosses the River Severn for the second time at Atcham.

Plate 84 An example of standard road furniture, 'Holyhead 104 miles' (*Derrick Beckett*)

Location No 15: Atcham Bridge
The A5(T) at Atcham is carried across the River Severn on a reinforced-concrete arch bridge constructed in 1929. The repair work that has been carried out to the concrete can be clearly seen and the bridge is about halfway through its design life of 120 years (see Montford Bridge, Chapter 3). Close by is the original bridge with seven circular stone arches (see Plate 22, p61), built by John Gwynn between 1768 and 1776. There is a marked contrast between the hump-backed form of Gwynn's design and Telford's designs for his Severn bridges.

Location No 16: Toll-house, Burcot
Burcot toll-house, a single-storey structure, is about three miles east of Atcham travelling towards Wellington. The tour now departs from the A5(T) and to avoid the network of roads round Telford and the M54, proceed along the B4380 to Ironbridge. At the approaches to Ironbridge there is a riverside park and parking area. Continue into Ironbridge and there is a car park a short distance beyond the bridge.

Location No 17: Ironbridge
Allow about one hour to visit the bridge (see Plate 23, p62) — the first
iron bridge in the world, cast at Coalbrookdale in 1779. There is an
information centre and exhibition in the toll-house at the south end of
the bridge. The bridge is the central feature of the Ironbridge Gorge
Museum, which spreads over an area of about six square miles. To visit
all the sites, it would be necessary to extend the tour by at least one day.
For further information on the Museum and its activities, in particular
the extensive collection of material on Telford's public works, contact
The Ironbridge Gorge Museum Trust, Ironbridge, Telford, Salop TF8
7AW (Tel: 095 245 3522 weekdays, or 095 245 3418 weekends). The
Skelton toll-house (1829) (see Chapter 4) with furnishings dating from
the second half of the nineteenth century, stands in Blists Hill Open Air
Museum, which forms part of the Ironbridge Gorge Museum complex.

Location No 18: St Michael's Church, Madeley
There are two Telford churches in the vicinity of Ironbridge, the
nearest being at Madeley (see Plate 6, p38). From Ironbridge, follow
the road to Madeley (A4169) and the church with its square tower can
be seen at the top of the hill. The church is signposted; follow Church
Street for about one mile. It was described by Telford as a 'very peculiar
construction'!

Location No 19: St Mary's Church, Bridgnorth
From Madeley, follow the signposts to Coalport and then turn on to the
A442 to Bridgnorth. At the approaches to Bridgnorth the church tower
and dome can be seen at the top of the hill on the right-hand side of the
road. On entering Bridgnorth, cross the River Severn and turn left. A
short distance on there is a sharp right-hand fork (signposted to town
centre). Follow this road up the hill with the castle remains on the right
and then turn right into East Castle Street. The church is at the end of
the street. The remainder of the fourth day of the tour involves following the route of the River Severn, south from Bridgnorth to Gloucester,
about 60 miles (100km) to inspect the bridges at Bewdley, Holt Fleet,
Mythe and Gloucester.

Location No 20: Bewdley Bridge
From Bridgnorth, continue on the A442 travelling south towards
Kidderminster. At the roundabout on the outskirts of Kidderminster,
turn right following the signposts to Bewdley. Cross over the bridge and
turn immediately left on to the road which runs parallel to the river. The
bridge, completed in 1799, is an elegant example of Telford's use of the

masonry arch and is visually the most attractive of his bridges over the River Severn (see Plate 28, p68).

Location No 21: Holt Fleet Bridge
The route from Bewdley is southwards via the B4194 towards Stourport-on-Severn and Astley Cross. Proceed from the B4194 to the B4196 and at Holt Heath turn left on to the A4133 to reach the bridge. Although it was opened in 1826, the 150ft (46m) span bridge still carries main road traffic. It was strengthened in 1928 and Plate 32 (see p70), taken in August 1984 when some maintenance was in progress, clearly shows the concrete casing of the soffit ironwork which in turn is reflected in the water.

Location No 22: Mythe Bridge
Mythe Bridge, about 25 miles (40km) downstream from Holt Heath, is the largest — 170ft (52m) — of Telford's single-span cast-iron bridges and, as with Holt Fleet Bridge, was opened in 1826. Proceed over Holt Fleet Bridge along the A4133 for about 2 miles (3.2km) and turn right at the roundabout on the outskirts of the village of Ombersley to join the A469(T). Follow the A469(T) to junction 6 on the M5 and proceed south down the M5 to junction 8. At junction 8, turn right on to the M50, and at junction 1 turn left and follow the A38(T) towards Tewkesbury. About 2 miles (3.6km) on, Mythe Bridge with its picturesque toll-house (see Plate 31, p70) is to be found at the junction of the A38(T) and the A438. Note also the narrow pointed flood arches (see Plate 30, p70). A concrete deck was added in 1923. To inspect the last of Telford's bridges over the River Severn, it is necessary to travel a further 15 miles (24km) to Gloucester.

Location No 23: Over Bridge, Gloucester
Proceed along the A438 into Tewkesbury and join the M5 at junction 9. Continue south down the M5 to junction 11 and then turn right on to the A40(T) and proceed through Gloucester, negotiating four round-abouts following the A40(T) signs. On the outskirts of Gloucester, Over Bridge can be seen in splendid isolation. It has now been bypassed, but until recently carried the A40(T) in spite of settlement problems (see Chapter 2). Over Bridge was opened in 1830 and the bevelled form of the elliptical stone arch should be noted (see Plate 34, p74).

This completes the England and Wales tour with the exception of the return journey to London, which takes about 2½ hours, 100 miles (176km). The most direct route is to follow the A40(T) to Oxford, about

50 miles (80km). It is then a further 10 miles (16km) to the junction of the A40(T) and the M40. Join the M40 at junction 7 (Great Milton) and proceed to junction 1 at Denham. Rejoin the A40(T) at Denham and proceed into the centre of London. The total distance from junction 7 of the M40 to the centre of London is about 50 miles (80km).

Tour 3: Scotland

At least seven days should be allowed for a tour by car of the Lowlands and Highlands if the start is made at London. In order to photograph the locations, the author and his travelling companion left London at 5.30am on Saturday 28 September 1985, returning to London the following Saturday at about 6pm. Overnight stops were made at Langholm (day 1), Dunkeld (day 2), Fort William (days 3 to 6) and Langholm (day 7). There is no time to take in other attractions of Scotland.

Leaving London about 5.30am on day one, it is possible to reach Langholm by about 1pm (using a small car: Renault 4). Take the M1 out of London and join the M6 at junction 19. Follow the M6 to the last junction on the M6, junction 44 just north of Carlisle. Join the A7(T) and proceed to Langholm about 18 miles (29km) from junction 44. The Eskdale Hotel (Tel: 0541 80357) provides comfortable accommodation and good food and is conveniently situated in the centre of the town.

Plate 85 The stone doorway built by Telford when working as an apprentice stonemason in Langholm (*Derrick Beckett*)

Plate 86 Langholm Bridge, the stonework is in excellent condition *(Derrick Beckett)*

Location No 1: Langholm

There is a Tourist Information Office across the road from the Eskdale Hotel (summer opening only) and Mr Harkness is most helpful with regard to local history and in particular Telford's works in and around Langholm. Adjacent to the Tourist Information Office is Langholm Library, which was instituted in 1800 and partially endowed by Telford (see inscription on the stone and Plate 20, p59). There is also the stone doorway (Plate 85) built by Telford when working as an apprentice mason in the Eskdale area. Walk back past the Eskdale Hotel down the hill to the north end of the town and then turn left to cross Eskdale Bridge. Turn left again and walk down the grass bank to the west abutment of the bridge. When the river level is low, it is possible to walk under the western arch — trousers rolled up to knee height. A number of Telford's mason's marks can still be seen and the stonework is in excellent condition (built c1775) (Plate 86). A fine distant view of the bridge with a gentle slope from east to west can be obtained from the suspension bridge a few hundred feet downstream. Note the sensitivity of this bridge to vibrations as pedestrians pass over it. It is possible to return to the Eskdale Hotel by crossing over the suspension bridge and walking up a side street to the centre of the town.

Plate 87 The graveyard and mausoleum at Westerkirk (*Derrick Beckett*)

Location No 2: Eskdale and Meggat Water

It is recommended that Sheet 79 of the Ordnance Survey Landranger Series (Harwick and Eskdale) is consulted prior to visiting the Telford Memorial, John Telford's headstone and Crooks Cottage. The round trip is about 20 miles (36km) and there is ample time in the summer months to complete the visit on the first day of the tour. (To reach Dunkeld on the second day an early start is required.) Proceed over Eskdale Bridge down Telford Road and follow the B709 to the Telford Memorial, which is shown on OS Sheet 79. Cross the road and walk to the back of the village school, with the library to the left. The view across to the River Esk (see Plate 21, p59) soon negates the tension of several hours of motorway driving earlier in the day. Westerkirk Church at Bentpath can be seen in the distance, just beyond the masonry arch crossing the river. Proceed along the B709 to Bentpath and turn left, crossing over the bridge and then turn immediately right. Westerkirk Church is on the left. The disused graveyard is a short distance up the road and the domed roof of the mausoleum of the Johnstones of Westerhall (see page 31) can be seen projecting above the perimeter stone wall. Walk round the perimeter wall and the entrance gate is at the top of the incline. Looking down from the entrance gate (Plate 87), John Telford's gravestone (see Plate 2, p34) is a few feet to the left of the corner of the mausoleum: 'In Memory of John Telford who, after living 33 years as an Unblameable Shepherd, Died at Glendinning, 12 November 1757 his son Thomas who died an infant' (the meaning of the last seven words is not clear). Time permitting, return to the church instead of turning left to re-cross the bridge, and continue straight on, with the new graveyard on the right. The road follows the line of the River Esk and a fork is reached where the road crosses Meggat Water. Do not cross the bridge, but bear right and proceed along the road which follows Meggat Water up to Glendinning. Speaking to a local, there appears to be some controversy over the exact location of Telford's birthplace and the cottage in which he subsequently lived. In Plate 3 (see p34) 'Crooks' as marked on OS Sheet 79 can be seen on the left and Meggat Water, out of camera range, to the right. The view is taken looking down towards the River Esk. In fading light, and with some reluctance the return journey was made to Langholm.

Location No 3: Cartland Crags Bridge, Lanark

On the second day of the tour, the first stage is a 70 mile (112km) drive from Langholm to Lanark. From Langholm, take the B7063 to Lockerbie, about 15 miles (24km). This is a scenic drive. At Lockerbie, proceed north along the A74(T) towards Glasgow for about 40 miles (64km). Note the gradients and alignment, the result of Telford's earlier work on the Glasgow and Carlisle road (see page 135). At the junction with the A70, turn right and proceed for about six miles (10km), and the A7(T) crosses the River Clyde at Hyndford Bridge (dated 1773); it remains as built, but is obviously not a Telford design. On crossing the bridge, follow the A73(T) through Lanark down the hill, with Cartland Bridge Hotel on the right. There is a sharp bend in the road where it crosses Mouse Water via Cartland Crags Bridge. It is possible to park in a small clearing on the right of the original toll-house. The view shown in Plate 69 (see p138) is taken from the edge of the clearing. The owners of the toll-house kindly gave the author permission to inspect the bridge from their garden, though it was all but obscured by trees clinging to the steep banks of the valley.

Location No 4: Dunkeld Bridge

The 80 mile (128km) drive from Lanark to Dunkeld is amply rewarded not only by the sight of Telford's elegant seven-span arch bridge but also the opportunity to cross the 3,300ft (1,006m) span Forth Suspension Bridge, downstream of which can be seen the majestic railway bridge. The railway bridge has an immense physical presence and when completed in 1889 had the world's largest main span of 1,710ft (521m).

From Cartland Crags Bridge, return to the centre of Lanark and pro-

ceed along the A706 for about 20 miles and join the M8 at junction 4.
Follow the M8 to junction 1 and then the signposts to the Forth Bridge.
On crossing the bridge, proceed along the M90 to junction 11 on the
outskirts of Perth. The M90 links with the A9(T) and Dunkeld is about
15 miles (24km) along the A9(T), travelling north in the direction of
Pitlochry. Dunkeld and Birnam are on a loop road to the right of the
A9(T). The Atholl Arms Hotel, Dunkeld (Tel: 035 02 219), once a
coaching inn, provides a comfortable overnight stop and stands at the
head of Telford's bridge, looking across the River Tay to Birnam
Wood. The hotel car park is adjacent to the bridge. Walk under the approach arch and there is a pleasant riverside walk from which the
subtlety of Telford's proportioning of the arches can be fully appreciated — a perfect demonstration of the art of engineering.

Location No 5: Fort William and Fassfern
About half of the third day of the tour involves a 90 mile (144km) drive
through the Scottish Highlands to Fort William. To appreciate the
scenery, a leisurely pace is recommended. From Dunkeld, rejoin the
A9(T) and proceed via Pitlochry; Blair Atholl and Glen Garry to Dal-
whinnie. Fork left on to the A889. The A889 joins the A86 at Drum-
gask; follow the signpost to Fort William. The A86 runs along the shore
of Loch Laggan which provides an appropriate 'aperitif' to lochs forming two-thirds of the length of the Caledonian Canal. Continue along the
A86 to the junction with the A82(T) at Spean Bridge. Follow the
A82(T) into Fort William. There is a wide choice of hotels and guest
houses in and around Fort William and reference should be made to the
Scottish Tourist Board publication. Allowing a full morning for the
journey from Dunkeld to Fort William, a leisurely hour or so can be
spent visiting a minor Telford bridge at Fassfern, which is in complete
contrast to the Tay crossing at Dunkeld. From Fort William, take the
A830(T) road to Mallaig; about 5 miles (8km) along the shores of Loch
Eil, Fassfern is on a loop road to the right of the A830(T). This bridge is
typical of several hundred minor bridges built over a period of 20 years
and has survived a constant and fast flowing stream (see Plate 72, p145),
carrying with it boulders and uprooted trees. It is worth continuing a
similar distance from Fassfern to Glenfinnan at the head of Loch Spiel.
It is here that Robert MacAlpine ('Concrete Bob') constructed the first
major concrete railway viaduct in Great Britain, c1898. This bridge has
no reinforcing steel and is a series of plain concrete arches in the spirit of
classical masonry construction. The railway line from Fort William to
Mallaig follows the route of the old Telford road.

Location Nos 6, 7 and 8: Invermoriston Bridge, WhiteBridge and Beauly Bridge

It is suggested that the fourth day of the tour is devoted to a 180 mile (290km) round trip to visit three bridges, but will also enable the scale of the Great Glen of Scotland to be fully appreciated, with numerous glimpses of the Caledonian Canal and Loch Lochy, Loch Oich and Loch Ness. Take the A82(T) from Fort William to Spean Bridge where it bears left to hug the eastern shore of Loch Lochy for about 8 miles (13km). The A82(T) crosses the Caledonian Canal between Loch Lochy and Loch Oich and then continues via Invergarry to Fort Augustus, crossing the canal again at Aberchalder. The canal is crossed for the third time at Fort Augustus and the A82(T) then follows the shore of Loch Ness to Invermoriston. Telford's bridge (see Plate 74, p146), a two-span masonry arch (disused), can be seen to the left shortly before the junction with the A887. There is an interesting rock formation on either side of the bridge with the Glen Garry forest in the background. From Invermoriston, return to Fort Augustus, cross the canal and follow the B862, which skirts the southern end of Loch Ness. The difference in alignment of the B862, a General Wade road (see Introduction) and Telford's roads, is immediately apparent. General Wade's humpbacked bridge (Whitebridge) crosses the River Fechlin and is about a 10

Plate 88 A typical General Wade hump-backed bridge, Whitebridge (1732) (*Derrick Beckett*)

mile (16km) drive from Fort Augustus. It has now been bypassed but can be seen to the right of the B862 as it crosses the river (Plate 89). From Whitebridge, follow the B862 and then the B852 along the shore of Loch Ness to Inverness, about 25 miles (40km). At Inverness, cross the River Ness and the Caledonian Canal at Muirtown and follow the A862 along the Beauly Firth, and Beauly (Lovat) Bridge is about 10 miles (16km) from Inverness. The five-span sandstone arch structure has recently been subjected to extensive repairs. Cracks up to 4in (100mm) developed as a result of stress and frost and there has been extensive stitching of the masonry with stainless steel tie-bars. The bridge is not only a listed structure, but also a scheduled ancient monument. Take the return journey to Fort William via the A862 and the A82(T).

Location No 9: Caledonian Canal
Days 5 and 6 should be allocated to the Caledonian Canal, which extends for a total of 60 miles (96km) between Fort William and Inverness. Starting from Fort William, take the A830(T) route as for Fassfern. After crossing the River Lochy and the canal (a swing bridge) turn right on to the B8004 signposted to Banavie. Adjacent to the Moorings Hotel there is a large circular parking area, at the back of which some steps lead up to the flight of eight locks (Neptune's Staircase). The view shown in Plate 59 (see p124) is taken from the bottom of the flight on the Fort William side of the canal. Walk up to the top and the bay windowed houses (see Plate 60, p124) can be seen on the hotel side of the locks (see Chapter 7). At the top of the flight there is a fine view of Ben Nevis (weather permitting). Continue along the B8004 towards Gairlochy and the road rises to a level at which it is possible to observe the route of the canal and the River Lochy below (see Plate 61, p126). At Gairlochy, walk along the towpath past the second lock, and between this lock and the lighthouse at the entrance to Loch Lochy there is a picturesque basin with conifers planted down to the water's edge (see Plate 62, p127). Continue along the B8004 and turn left on to the A82(T), then follow the same route but stop at Laggan to inspect the two locks. Proceed along the A82(T) to Aberchalder, where the road crosses the River Oich and the Caledonian Canal. Note also the rusting suspension bridge, not a Telford design. To obtain a true impression of the scale of the canal, an hour's walk along the canal from Aberchalder towards Fort William is recommended. At Fort Augustus there is a flight of five locks and the Great Glen Heritage Exhibition at the swing bridge is worth a visit. It covers the history of the area, including forestry, the Caledonian Canal and Bonnie Prince Charlie (open May to October, admission free). Return to Fort William via the A82(T). On the sixth day,

allow time to walk up one of the numerous tracks at the side of Loch Ness on the A82(T) between Invermoriston and Drumnadrochit. Those willing to climb high above the loch will be amply rewarded by the view. For the final stage, proceed to Inverness and follow the A862 to Muirtown, where the canal is crossed by a swing bridge. There is a flight of four locks at Muirtown and a number of interesting boats are moored in the large basin (see Plate 65, p130). Follow the A862 a short distance on; the Canal Office is on the left, with Robert Southey's tribute to Telford inscribed on a stone slab. It is possible to park on the opposite side of the road alongside the canal workshops and the lock referred to as the Works Lock. Walk past the lock and cross the railway adjacent to the swing bridge which carries the railway over the canal. The cable-stayed bridge (Kessock Bridge) which takes the A9(T) over the entrance to the Beauly Firth can be seen in the distance, but even more impressive is the view along the artificial banks to the sea lock some 1,200ft (370m) beyond the shore line (see Plate 67, p131). Return to Fort William via the A82(T). On the seventh day, return to Langholm using the shorter route via Glasgow: A82, M74, A74 and B7063 at Lockerbie. An overnight stay at Langholm allows some time for further exploration of Eskdale.

The return journey to London — A74, M6, M1 — will occupy most of the eighth day. A diversion for the enthusiastic is a visit to the British Waterways Board's Waterways Museum, which stands beside the Grand Union Canal at Stoke Bruerne. Leave the M1 at junction 15 and proceed for about 4 miles (6.4km) along the A508 towards Stony Stratford. Just before the A508 crosses the canal, turn right into Stoke Bruerne, and at the top of the museum car park one of the cast-iron ribs which originally supported the first section of Telford's Pont Cysyllte Aqueduct can be inspected (see Chapter 3).

The museum was opened in 1963 and attracts more than 100,000 visitors a year. In spite of the inevitable commercialism, Stoke Bruerne, situated in the heart of the peaceful Northamptonshire countryside, retains much of the character of a village in the previous century. The exhibits are housed on three floors of what was once a large grain warehouse, which was powered by a steam engine mounted in an adjacent building. The exhibits present a fascinating insight into many aspects of two centuries of canal life. The entrance to Blisworth Tunnel, the largest tunnel still in use on the waterways system, is only a short walk along the towing path.

The exhibition space available, although cleverly utilised, cannot possibly do justice to the story of the canal age of commerce and industry founded on reliable water transport in canal and river navigations.

Hopefully, this situation will shortly change, as it has been announced that a National Waterways Museum is to be established in the historic Llanthany Warehouse at Gloucester Docks. The plans for the museum have been approved by the Secretary of State for the Department of the Environment, with an opening date scheduled for 1988. The space available will be over ten times that at Stoke Bruerne and this £3.5 million project will give the National Waterways Museum Trust, who are to establish and run the museum, the opportunity to stimulate further interest in inland waterways.

In particular, it is proposed to include the reproduction of a lock under repair and a section through a typical waterway. As we have seen, the civil engineering aspects of canal construction are largely hidden by water or soil.

Although Telford was not involved with the construction of the Llanthany Warehouse — it was opened in 1874 — he was connected, through the Exchequer Loan Commission (see p45), with the completion of the Gloucester and Berkeley Canal. The canal was authorised by an Act of 1793 and it was designed to avoid navigation problems associated with the lower reaches of the River Severn. The project was beset with financial and administrative problems and in 1817, following Telford's recommendation, work proceeded on a shorter route which joined the Severn Estuary at Sharpness. It was eventually completed in 1827 and still carries goods traffic: it was classified as a commercial waterway under the Transport Act of 1968. Telford's major association with Gloucester is, of course, Over Bridge with its 'cornes de vache' (see Chapter 2). Visitors to the new museum will have the opportunity to inspect this bridge and others designed by Telford to cross the River Severn, exemplifying his immense contribution to the development of navigable waterways.

TECHNICAL APPENDIX — SUSPENSION AND ARCH BRIDGES

A simple mathematical treatment of the suspension bridge is given in the Technical Appendix to *Brunel's Britain*, and by considering the arch as an inversion of the suspension chain, equations common to both systems can be derived. A typical arrangement of the components of a suspension bridge is shown in Fig 19(a). If the intensity of vertical loading w of the deck is uniform along its length and the weight of the chain is small compared with the deck, then the geometrical form of the chain approximates to that of a parabola. Consider the equilibrium of one half of the main span of the chain (Fig 19(b)); then

$$H. \ h \ = \ \frac{wL}{2}. \frac{L}{4}$$

$$H \ = \ \frac{wL^2}{8h} \qquad\qquad \text{(equation 1)}$$

Equation 1 gives the tension in the chain at the centre of the main span. For horizontal equilibrium, the horizontal component of the tension T in the chain is constant, and thus at the tower the value of the tension becomes

$$T \ = \ (H^2 + V^2)^{1/2}$$

where
$$V \ = \ \frac{wL}{2} \qquad \text{[the vertical reaction at the tower from the main span.]}$$

$$\text{Thus } T \ = \ \left[\left(\frac{wL^2}{8h}\right)^2 + \left(\frac{wL}{2}\right)^2 \right]^{1/2}$$

$$= \ \frac{wL^2}{8h} \left[1 + 16 \left(\frac{h}{L}\right)^2 \right]^{1/2} \qquad \text{(equation 2)}$$

A typical value of the ratio dip h to the span L is 0.1, and for this value the tension in the chain at the tower becomes

$$T \ = \ \frac{wL^2}{8h} \left[1 + 0.16 \right]^{1/2}$$

$$= \ 1.08 \frac{wL^2}{8h}$$

This represents an 8 per cent increase on the value

$$H \ = \ \frac{wL^2}{8h}$$

at the centre of the main span. It can also be shown that the length of the chain Lc approximates to

$$Lc = L \left[1 + \frac{8}{3} \left(\frac{h}{L}\right)^2\right] \qquad \text{(equation 3)}$$

Again, if $\frac{h}{L} = 0.1$ then $Lc = 1.03L$, a small increase on the horizontal span L between the towers.

For the Menai Suspension Bridge, the horizontal distance between the towers is 580ft (177m) and the dip 43ft (13m). Working in metric units, let the area of the chains be A; if the unit weight of the metal approximates to 76 kN/m³, then the weight per unit length of the chains is 76A. As an approximation, consider this to be constant over the length L; then the tension due to the weight of the chains alone is approximately

$$H = \frac{(76A)L^2}{8h}$$

The intensity of load per unit area (stress) in the chains is given by

$$f = \frac{H}{A}$$

$$= \frac{76L^2}{8h}$$

$$= \frac{76.177^2}{8.13}$$

$$= 22894 \, kN/m^2$$

$$= 22.89 \, N/mm^2 \, (1.5 \, tons/in^2)$$

For Telford's proposed design for the Runcorn Bridge with L = 1000ft (306m) and h = 50ft (15.3m), the value of f increases to 58.1N/mm² (3.81T/in²). Cast iron is unreliable in tension, ie extension of the material fibres, and permissible stresses for the full design load — chains, hangers, deck, vehicle and pedestrian loading — are given in Table 6.

Table 6   London Building Act (1909) permissible working stresses

	Tons/in²	*N/mm²*
Cast iron		
Tension	1.5	23
Compression	8.0	124
Shearing	1.5	23
Bearing	10.0	154
Wrought iron		
Tension	5.0	77
Compression	5.0	77
Shearing	4.0	62
Bearing	7.0	108
Mild steel		
Tension	7.5	116
Compression	7.5	116
Shearing	5.5	85
Bearing	11.0	170

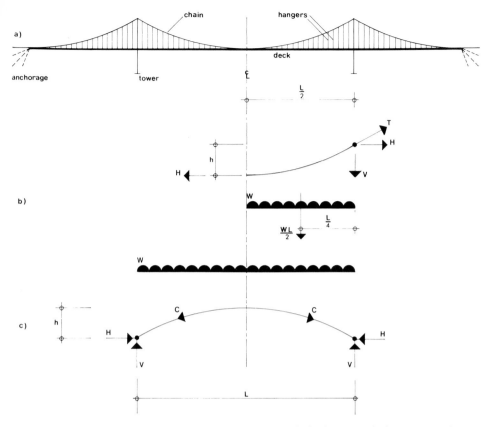

Fig 19a) The components of a suspension bridge — chain, hangers, deck, towers and anchorage
b) Equilibrium of the half chain
c) Arch considered as the inverse of the chain

Thus the unsuitability of cast iron for suspension bridges is immediately apparent (tension 23N/mm²) and the difference between values for cast iron and those for wrought iron and steel is most significant.

Equations 1 and 2 can be used to estimate the thrust (compression) in a parabolic arch under uniformly distributed load as in Fig 19(c). From the table it can be seen that permissible compressive stresses for cast iron are much greater than the tension values, thus indicating the appropriateness of cast iron for use in the arch form as demonstrated so admirably by Telford – Bonar, Craigellachie, Waterloo, Holt Fleet and Mythe bridges, and the proposals for crossing the Thames and the Menai Strait.

However, this simple mathematical treatment relates to a static uniformly distributed loading — an illusion. The passage of a moving load across the deck of a suspension bridge causes continuous alteration to the shape of the chain, resulting in deformation and oscillation of the roadway. To accept moving loads of any magnitude and to resist wind loading a suspension bridge must be stiffened to ensure that it maintains its shape. This is normally achieved by using a deep trussed girder to stiffen the deck, as with the reconstructed Menai Bridge (1940). In recent British designs, a shallow steel box girder has been

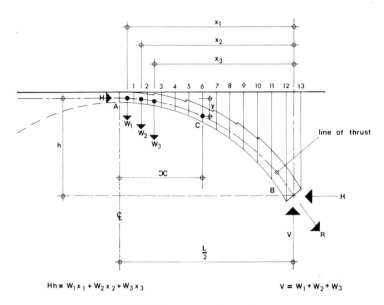

$$Hh = W_1 x_1 + W_2 x_2 + W_3 x_3 \qquad\qquad V = W_1 + W_2 + W_3$$

Fig 20 The momentless arch

used, eg Severn and Humber bridges. As we have seen, the light timber deck of the original Telford design for the Menai Bridge suffered damage in a gale shortly after the bridge was opened and was replaced by a stronger deck in 1839 (see Chapter 3).

Analogous to the change in shape of a suspension chain for different loading conditions, loading on a parabolic arch, rather than the uniformly distributed load discussed previously, will result in a non-uniform stress distribution across the arch voussoirs. It is possible to develop an arch profile such that under the action of the weight of voussoirs, spandrels and deck, the arch rib will be under uniform compression — referred to as a momentless arch. The half arch can be divided into vertical sections (see Fig 20) and the weight of each section W_1, W_2 etc, estimated. If at any point C, a horizontal distance x from the arch centre line, the bending effect due to the thrust H times the distance y is made equal to the opposite bending effect due to the loads W_1, W_2 etc, to the left of C, then the bending effect is zero and the thrust induces a uniform compressive stress over the depth of the rib. At the arch springing, point B, we have the result

$$H.h = W_1 x_1 + W_2 x_2 + \ldots$$

For any other loading, the line of action of the arch thrust will shift, resulting in stress distributions typically shown in Fig 21. For a rectangular cross section, there will be zero stress on one face and twice the uniform stress f on the other face when the line of thrust shifts by an amount equal to one-sixth the depth of the section. Until recently, it was thought that the safety of an arch depended on keeping the line of action of the arch thrust within a distance of D/6 on either side of the centre of the section, the so-called middle third rule. If the shift of the line of action of thrust exceeds D/6, then the above theory will predict tension and the voussoirs will attempt to separate (see Fig 21d). It was then assumed that the thrust acts on a reduced section depth with a corresponding increase in compressive stress (Fig 21e).

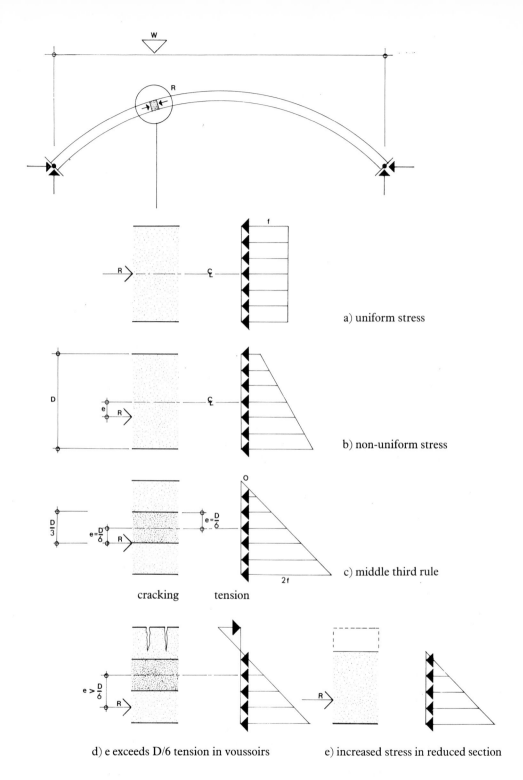

a) uniform stress

b) non-uniform stress

c) middle third rule

cracking   tension

d) e exceeds D/6 tension in voussoirs   e) increased stress in reduced section

Fig 21 The middle third rule

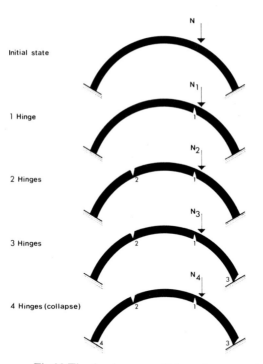

Initial state

1 Hinge

2 Hinges

3 Hinges

4 Hinges (collapse)

Fig 22 The development of hinges in a voussoir arch

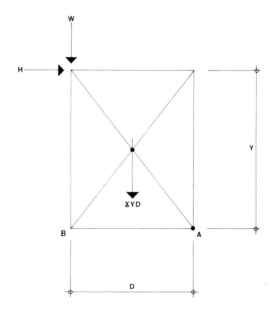

Fig 23 The stability of a rigid block

Experimental and theoretical work in the twentieth century (A. J. S. Pippard, J. Heyman) has resulted in a better understanding of the mechanics of the voussoir arch (see Fig 22). Consider the application of a steadily increasing load to a voussoir arch. Initially, at a load N_1, the voussoirs will remain in contact. Increasing the load to N_2 will cause joint 1 to open, forming a so-called hinge. With further increase in load, additional hinges will be formed at joints 2 and 3. At a load N_4, a fourth hinge will form and the arch becomes a mechanism and will collapse. The existing stock of arches on our road network is in the order of 100,000 and thus there is currently great interest in the assessment of these bridges, many of which are over 100 years old. The requirement of a 120 year life has been mentioned previously and the voussoir arch has admirably demonstrated its durability, exemplified by Telford's bridge over the River Severn at Montford (1792).

A simple treatment of the abutment to an arch is to consider it as a rigid block (J. Heyman). Let H be the arch thrust and W the half weight of the arch for unit width (see Fig 23). If the abutment has a width D and height Y for unit width, and the unit weight of the material is γ, then by ignoring the weight of the half arch and taking moments about A

$$H.Y = (\gamma YD).\frac{D}{2}$$

$$D = \left(\frac{2H}{\gamma}\right)^{1/2} \qquad \text{(equation 4)}$$

This is a reasonable approximation if the weight of the abutment is large compared with the half arch. The value of D obtained from equation 4 is that required to prevent overturning by rotation about point A. A further consideration is sliding of the block along the line BA. If the coefficient of friction between the block and the ground is μ, then $\mu\gamma DY$ must be greater than H.

Further Reading

Heyman, J. *The Masonry Arch* (Ellis Horwood Ltd, 1982)

Heyman, J. 'Calculation of abutment sizes for masonry arches' (International Association for Bridge & Structural Engineering (British Group) Colloquium on History of Structures, Pembroke College, Cambridge, July 1982)

Pippard, A. J. S., Tranter, E. and Chitty, L. 'The mechanics of the voussoir arch' (Journal of the Institution of Civil Engineers, December 1936)

Pugsley, A. *The Safety of Structures* (Edward Arnold, 1966)

BIBLIOGRAPHY

A comprehensive collection of material on Thomas Telford is held at the Iron-bridge Gorge Museum, Ironbridge Gorge Museum Trust, Ironbridge, Telford, Salop TF8 7AW. In addition to the collection, which is on microfilm, there is a teaching unit on Telford which provides a useful introduction to Telford's life and works. Robert Southey's *Journal of a Tour in Scotland in 1819* is a fascinating contemporary account of Telford's works in Scotland and is extensively quoted in the text. Of at least equal interest are Southey's observations on social and industrial conditions in Scotland in the early years of the nineteenth century. L.T.C. Rolt's biography of Thomas Telford is written in an elegant style and is essential reading. To the author, the *Atlas to the life of Thomas Telford, Civil Engineer, containing eighty-three copper plates illustrative of his professional labour* does more than any words to demonstrate the quality of Telford's work.

Beckett, D. *Brunel's Britain* (David & Charles, 1980)

Beckett, D. *Great Buildings of the World, Bridges* (Paul Hamlyn, 1969)

Beckett, D. *Stephensons' Britain* (David & Charles, 1984)

Birmingham Canal Navigations. (Traffic Education Publications Birmingham, 1977)

Bracegirdle, B. and Miles, P. H. *Great Engineers and their works, Thomas Telford* (David & Charles, 1973)

Cameron, A. D. *Getting to Know . . . The Caledonian Canal* (A. D. Cameron, Edinburgh, 1982)

Cameron, A. D. *Thomas Telford and the Transport Revolution* (Longman, 1979)

Cohen, P. 'Origins of the Pont Cysyllte Aqueduct' (Transactions of the Newcomen Society, Vol 51, 1979–80)

Cossons, N. and Trinder, B. *The Iron Bridge* (Moonraker Press, 1979)

Danby, J. 'Preserving integrity and appearance' (Construction Repairs and Maintenance, March 1986)

Dobson, E. *Foundations and Concrete Works circa 1850* (John Wale 1850; reprinted by Kingsmead Reprints, Bath, 1970)

Gagg, J. *Canals in a Nutshell* (John Gagg, Princes Risborough, 1977)

Gibb, A. *The Story of Telford* (Alexander Maclehose, London, 1935)

Hadfield, C. and Skempton, A. W. *William Jessop, Engineer* (David & Charles, 1979)

Heyman, J. and Threfall, B. P. 'Two Masonry Bridges: II. Telford's bridge at Over' (Proceedings of the Institution of Civil Engineers, Vol 52, November 1972)

Horsnell, B. C. *St. Katharine Docks, Yacht Haven and World Trade Centre* (Handell Ltd, 1982)

Kemp, E. L. *Links in a Chain, The Development of Suspension Bridges 1801–70* (The Structural Engineer, vol 57A, No 8, August 1979)

Maunsell, G. A. 'Menai Bridge Reconstruction' (Journal of the Institution of Civil Engineers, January, 1946)

Nicholson *The Ordnance Survey Guide to the Waterways, 2 Central* (Robert Nicholson Publications Ltd, 1983)

Parsons, W. B. *Engineers and Engineering in the Renaissance* (The MIT Press, 1968)

Penfold, A. (editor) 'Thomas Telford: Engineer' (Proceedings of a seminar held at Ironbridge, April 1979, Thomas Telford Ltd, London, 1980) Contents are:

(i)   Lawson, J. B. 'Thomas Telford in Shrewsbury: the metamorphosis of an architect into a civil engineer'

(ii)   Clayton, A. R. K. 'The Shrewsbury and Newport Canals: construction and remains'

(iii)   Trinder, B. 'The Holyhead Road: an engineering project put in its social context'

(iv)   Skempton, A. W. 'Telford and the design for a new London Bridge'

(v)   Paxton, R. A. 'Menai Bridge, 1813–26, evaluation of design'

(vi)   Dalgleish, A. 'Telford's steam carriages'

(vii)   Penfold, A. 'Managerial organisation of the Caledonian Canal 1803–22'

(viii) Hume, J. R. 'Telford's Highland Bridges'

Pontydd *Menai and the Menai Bridges* (Welsh Arts Council and Gwynedd Archives Service, 1980)

Rolt, L. T. C. *Navigable Waterways* (revised edition, Penguin Books, 1985)

Rolt, L. T. C. *Thomas Telford* (first published by Longmans, 1958; Pelican Books, 1979)

Ruddock, T. *Arch Bridges and their Builders 1735–1835* (Cambridge University Press, 1979)

Singer, C. *et al. A History of Technology, volume 4, The Industrial Revolution (c. 1750 to c. 1850)* (The Clarendon Press, 1975)

Skempton, A. W. 'The engineers of the English river navigations, 1620–1760' (Transactions of the Newcomen Society, Vol 29, 1953–4)

Skempton, A. W. 'Engineering in the Port of London 1808–33' (Transactions of the Newcomen Society, Vol 53, 1981–2)

Smiles, S. *Lives of the Engineers, Volume III, History of Roads, Metcalf: Telford* (a new and revised edition, John Murray, London, 1874)

Smith, P. L. *Discovering Canals in Britain* (Shire Publications Ltd, 1981)

Southey, R. *Journal of a Tour in Scotland* (John Murray, London, 1929)

Syme, R. *The Story of Britain's Highways* (Pitman, 1952)

Telford, T. *Life of Thomas Telford* (ed. John Rickman, James and Luke G. Hansard, London 1838) Accompanied by the *Atlas to the life of Thomas Telford, Civil Engineer, containing eighty-three copper plates illustrative of his professional labours* (Sold by Payne & Foss, Pall Mall, 1838)

Tucker, M. 'St. Katharine Docks' (The Arup Journal, September, 1970)

Waterways World Guide *Llangollen Canal* (1981)

Waterways World Guide *Shropshire Union Canal* (1981)

Watson, J. G. *A Short History* (Institution of Civil Engineers, 1982)

ACKNOWLEDGEMENTS

I am greatly indebted to Malcolm Kaye for preparing the illustrations, maintaining the same quality and style as with *Brunel's Britain* and *Stephensons' Britain*. Gerry Raleigh undertook the tedious task of enlarging the photographs and I am grateful to Richard Jewell for photographing Waterloo Bridge at Betws-y-Coed at the eleventh hour, due to an unaccountable omission by the author. Paul and Margaret Marsh have provided constant support over the years and Paul kindly acted as chauffeur on a hectic tour of England and Wales in the summer of 1984. Jill and Robert Vickers have generously helped me through the final panic stages of completion of the text. Ted Fuller and Richard Packer kindly took the photographs of illustrations in *Telford's Atlas* and I am grateful for the permission of Kay Brooks to use the facilities of the Civil Engineering Department Library at Imperial College, London.

This work would not have been completed without the constant and loyal support of Sally, my wife, Stephen and Annie (Mumsie) Jewell and Ted Fuller. Sally accompanied me on a whirlwind eight-day photographic tour of Scotland which involved travelling over 1,500 miles in a Renault 4 van. Sally also typed the text, without (undue!) complaint, over numerous weekends.

Finally, I would like to acknowledge the co-operation of the partners and staff of Sir Frederick Snow & Partners and Jaqueline Mitchell of David & Charles Publishers in bringing this book to fruition.

INDEX